Skating on the Edge

Author's photo by E. David Luria

A child, taken from its home because of abuse or neglect, is just bewildered by what is happening to its world. Lawyers represent the interests of the state; other lawyers appear in court for the parents, but who stands to argue for the child?

The *Guardian ad Litem* program advocates for such children, insuring that their interests will remain paramount in the eyes of the court. It is staffed almost entirely by volunteers, and my late wife was one of them. Royalties from the sale of this book will be donated to the *Friends of the Guardian ad Litem* program.

ISBN: 1-4196-4902-7

To order additional copies, please contact us.
BookSurge, LLC
www.booksurge.com
1-866-308-6235
orders@booksurge.com

Skating on the Edge

A Memoir and Journey through a
Metamorphosis of the CIA

Carlos D. Luria

2006

Skating on the Edge

TABLE OF CONTENTS:

AUTHOR'S NOTE:

This work is first and foremost a memoir, but about one half of it is devoted to the CIA, which dominated my professional life. The Intelligence Community is probably the least well understood institution of the government – in part because of the secrecy with which it surrounds itself, but also because its practices are sometimes akin to sausage-making: just give us the end product, and spare us the details.

It is an institution that is sometimes politicized, sometimes misused, but remains an activity that no major power can do without. Because of its vulnerability to abuse, however, it is also an institution that requires sober, public scrutiny – by a diligent press, by a responsible Congress, by an independent Judiciary – and by an occasional whistleblower. Such scrutiny *may* compromise an approach we would rather keep secret, or a tactic that could aid an enemy; in my view, that is a risk a democracy must take --if it wishes to remain a democracy.

The Intelligence Community has changed dramatically over the past few years, because of the president's contention that he has the inherent right to use its tools in any way he chooses. Commenting on the Administration's legal defense of torture, the respected historian Arthur Schlesinger, Jr. observed: "No position taken has done more damage to America's reputation in the world – ever."

To Scott, Anne and Saissy...

... Every dad should be so lucky.

And to the memory of Sharon D. Luria, 1936 - 2006

PROLOGUE

"No, that's nonsense. That wasn't me. I mean, it wasn't I."

"But you *were* aboard the *SS President Roosevelt* in 1937, crossing to Europe? And you *were* nine years old?"

"Lady, Mrs. Hayden, whatever -- a lot of people were nine years old in 1937, and the vessel could have been the *Roosevelt* -- we went back and forth every year. But where is all this coming from, anyway?"

"My mother. She was 16 that year. She was on her way to Europe with her family. She says that you were a terror."

"A terror? Lady -- that's rubbish. She's talking about someone else. What makes her think it was me?"

"Your name was on the passenger list. And she has a picture."

As young people, we are not very interested in our heritage; we're so full of ourselves -- so convinced our elders have made a royal mess of the world, and that we will do much better. It isn't until we grow older that we begin to take an interest in our origins, and then, often, it is too late: the principals are dead; little pages of our history have vanished.

Mrs. Anne Hayden's phone call floored me, and she followed it up with a letter, extracts from her mother's diary -- *and* the incriminating photo.

"We spend our time trying to persuade him not to wreck the ship," Frances wrote in her diary. Why they didn't just heave the little bastard overboard is unclear, but had they done so, this account would not have been written.

A few years ago I served as a Hospice volunteer and spent some time reminiscing with a terminally ill patient. Eventually he told me that he had been a bombardier during World War II, had been shot down over Italy and been imprisoned by the Italians.

A rebellious sort, he was disciplined repeatedly, spent time in solitary but finally succeeded in escaping. He was recaptured and turned over to the Germans, managed to escape yet again, and hid in a peasant's barn.

The farmer's dog discovered him, however, and as the peasant and his wife began to sound the alarm, he killed them both, along with their dog. He stole some of the peasant's clothes, and headed south, toward the advancing Allied forces, and to safety.

"What a story. Have you shared this with your children?" He had not. The look of surprise on the peasant's face as the airman drove a pitch-fork through his throat; his wife's screams as she saw her husband collapse at her feet, choking on his own blood, and the abject terror in her eyes as he smashed her skull again and again, haunted him still -- sixty years later.

He had killed hundreds, maybe thousands, impersonally, from 10,000 ft. or more, but this was the first time he had killed face to face; he had never before talked about it to anyone. Yet he seemed relieved at having finally confronted his demons, and I persuaded him to let me bring a tape recorder to our next session.

That night he died, however, and his children and grandchildren never heard his story from his own lips.

I don't know very much about my father. I lived in his house for years, but never really got to know him. He was a dour, stiff-necked Prussian who rarely talked about himself, or his background. Only after his death did I discover that his reticence was a mixture of shyness and extreme modesty. Only then did I learn that he had served with such distinction in WW-I, that he had fought for Germany on the Russian front, and received innumerable decorations, including the Iron Cross. I learned that, in fact, from his commanding officer, who wrote me a letter of condolence at the time of my Dad's death.

When we sorted through his possessions, we came across his medals, tucked away in an old envelope and buried in a dusty file folder. He never got over the way his country had treated him -- a war hero he was, but he was also a Jew, and therefore destined for extermination. Had my American-born mother not handed him an ultimatum—told him that she was taking the children to the States, hoped he would come as well, but she, in any event, was leaving – he would have remained and perished in the Camps – as did his sister, and all of her family.

Yet he couldn't quite bring himself to throw the medals away. I knew he had been a prominent businessman in Hamburg. I knew that when he came to this country in his mid-forties, he had started all over again and had risen to the vice presidency of a medium-sized corporation. But that's about the extent of my knowledge.

What a shame. To his grandchildren and their offspring, he will always be a one-dimensional, shadowed figure in their background -- and they will be the poorer for it. I don't want that to continue. We need to know where we came from; we need to understand what forces in our background shaped the attitudes of our ancestors, dictated how we ourselves were raised, and influenced how we related to our own children. .

Years ago, when we returned from our first tour abroad, Martha and I were treated to a week at Lake Mohonk, a fine old Quaker resort in the Catskills that served tea in the afternoons while a string quartet played soothingly in the background. Our room overlooked a natural pool, and the mountains beyond, and every morning I took my little portable typewriter out on the balcony, determined to spend a solid three hours writing.

I made it through the Dedication and the Acknowledgements, but bogged down on page 1. In fact, after filling innumerable wastebaskets with crumpled "page 1's", I realized that serious writing was not my forte. I can write to a person, but not to a public. I can tailor stuff to friends (who are so gloriously forgiving), but not to an objective critic.

The trick, I suspect, is to publish posthumously. Posthumous is good. People are much more forgiving of the dead – *de mortui, nili bono*, and all that. Unless it is Bette Davis referring to Joan Crawford's death, of course: the two aging actresses were said to have hated one another, and the quote attributed to Ms. Davis when Joan Crawford died is: "You should never say anything but good about the dead. Joan Crawford is dead. Good! "

As this memoir grew, it developed a form of its own. The CIA years, covered in Chapter 3, required context and I began to include relevant historical vignettes of some of the Cold War's lesser known events.

Then 9/11 happened – unforeseen, and unquestionably the most devastating of a series of apparent Intelligence failures. That was followed by unfounded reports of Weapons of Mass Destruction (WMD's) the failure to anticipate the rise of the insurgents in Iraq, or to properly call the outcome of the Palestinian elections.

Where did it go wrong? How and why did it go wrong? How could agencies with budgets in the billions and staffs of exceptionally bright people have so badly failed to connect the dots?

Were these failures of the Intelligence professionals? Were they due to the mindset of an Administration unwilling to take the many warnings seriously? Or did they reflect an inherent set of weaknesses that plague *all* Intelligence Services -- that cannot be corrected by legislation or by reorganization, and that we simply have to learn to live with? I had to find the answer.

But there was more. 9/11 transformed the entire Intelligence Community in worrisome ways. The scandal of Abu Ghraib, the tales of torture at Guantanamo, the rumors of secret renditions to prisons in far off lands, the proliferation of massive wiretaps done without judicial review. Gradually at first and then at an accelerating pace, an Intelligence capability that once operated within limits a democracy could condone, became a blunt instrument for the raw projection of power. America was losing its moral compass; it was turning into just another global bully.

I had spent the 20 months prior to World War II in a British boarding school, and in early 2006 reconnected with one of my old classmates. He reminisced about his experiences during the buzz-bomb attacks on London:

"It wasn't the buzz that worried us," he said; "it was the silence."

"The silence?"

He shifted painfully in his chair; the arthritis in his hip made it difficult for him to remain in one position for long.

"The silence," he repeated, "preceded by a click. When we heard the click, we knew we had about 30 seconds to take cover." He shook his head, remembering – the images still sharp and clear, sixty years later.

"The buzz was tracked by some part of our brains, I suppose, but not on a conscious level. The click, however, would wake us from the deepest sleep, and the silence that followed became our total focus as we began the count-down: 30, 29, 28...

"If we weren't already spending the night in the bomb shelter, we scurried to hide under our beds, or took cover beneath a sturdy table, for even if it were the house down the street that took the hit, chunks of plaster were likely to break loose from our ceilings."

He moved again. His eyes took on a far away look as the memories raced across the synapses of his mind: the cries of anguish; the acrid smell of cordite and burning wood; the images of friends and neighbors pinned under the debris of their homes; their screams of pain no matter how gently they were pulled free. And all of that overlaid with the somber, bi-tonal wail of ambulances and fire engines, rushing to the scene.

He was talking about the V-1's that were flung at London for nine months - almost 10,000 of them in all. Unguided 'cruise missiles': 25' long; 4,000 lbs. fueled and armed, carrying over a ton of incendiaries and high explosives in their warheads, and with a range of 160 miles.

They were powered by a primitive jet engine that fired three or four bursts per second and produced the V-1's characteristic buzz. After a preset time, the fuel would shut off with a loud click, and the bomb would drop — wherever it happened to be at that moment. Russian roulette, replayed 35 times per day.

"You must have been terrified," I said. "You were — what — 15, 16?"

"I was 16 by then, and terrified is the right word. As well as surprised; we all were. The attacks began a couple of weeks *after* D-Day; we thought we had Jerry on the run. I was rigid with fear, because my Dad was off, fighting in France, and I wouldn't know whether my Mum and older sister had survived. They were all the family I had."

The V-1 was a terror weapon, pure and simple: Hitler's last, desperate attempt to break the will of a British people already exhausted by five years of war. Because they couldn't be aimed with any accuracy; they just dropped wherever they happened to be. In fact, fewer than 25% of them actually reached their destination.

"And the rest?"

"Some were shot down by Anti Aircraft batteries; some were intercepted by Spitfires; some became entangled in the barrage balloons over London and exploded harmlessly, and some were blown off course by wind gusts."

"How in God's name did you retain your sanity, going through this night after night, for nine months?"

"Some didn't. Some sank into deep depressions. Some drank themselves into a stupor every night. Our neighbor, Mrs. Hammersmith, attacked our air raid warden with a meat cleaver when he rushed to help her; she had to be led off in restraints."

But after a few weeks, life settled into a routine — what other choice was there? They tended their wounded. They buried their dead. They comforted their neighbors, and sheltered those whose homes had been destroyed. Churchill said of them: *"This was their Finest Hour."*

Contrast that to 9/11. We took a tremendous hit and lost 3,000 lives -- but it was over in a matter of hours; it didn't go on for months. 98% of New York City and 99.99% of the rest of the nation were unaffected by the attack.

Or think of the bomb plot foiled by the British in August of 2006. Even if all ten airliners had blown up in the skies, the casualties would have been far fewer than the 42,000 deaths, 2,788,000 injured and $23B in property damage we absorb _every year_ on our nation's highway[1], with no noticeable impact on our economy. Yet from the angst they spawned and from our reactions to them, you might think we had narrowly escaped Armageddon. Ours is an enormous country, with vast and redundant resources; of course we'd prefer to avoid terrorist attacks on our soil, but we could in fact absorb dozens of them with no appreciable effect, and still recover.

As did London.

And yet, because of them, we have all but abandoned our system of checks and balances, and seriously eroded our civil liberties. As historians look back upon this period, do you think they will say of us: *"This was their Finest Hour?"*

***

Chapter 3 was submitted to the CIA's Publications Review Board, which redacted some of the specific names and references, and which asked me to include the following disclaimer:

> All statements of fact, opinion or analysis expressed are those of the author and do not reflect the official positions or views of the CIA or any other US Government agency. Nothing in the contents should be construed as asserting or implying US Government authentication of information or Agency endorsement of the author's views. This material has been reviewed by the CIA to prevent the disclosure of classified information.

Which may be the appropriate point for entering a disclaimer of my own: As former colleagues and strict constructionists will find, I have taken some editorial liberties. I have simplified and truncated cases that were far more complex and convoluted than I make them appear. I have taken the memoirist's license of using pacing and humor to dramatize some events that in fact were rather prosaic, and on occasion I have let my liberal bias show through to a greater extent than is perhaps appropriate for an objective observer. But the essential facts are as reported. .

This account owes much to so many, and for their advice, their encouragement and their patience I am eternally grateful. I become testy and uncommunicative when I write, 'honeydo's' remained undone and a trail of crumbs and coffee stains bear testimony to my frequent trips to the kitchen. My wife, Sharon, put up with all of this with patience and good humor and more importantly, identified portions of the manuscript that would not have been clear to the average reader.

Lynne McKelvey in California was one of the first to view the draft and forced me to address the question: "for whom are you writing this stuff?"

Ruth Story Townsend, a master teacher and mentor *extraordinaire*, took the time to critique my effort and gently made me aware of its shortcomings. I enrolled in her course on writing memoirs and learned much about structure, dialogue and pacing.

My daughter, Sarah Luria, a distinguished professor of American Literature at Holy Cross University and author of the critically acclaimed *Capital Speculations*, made me tighten the manuscript's focus, clarify the historical references and clean up the detritus of careless writing.

Geoffrey Rowson, a classmate from my British schooldays, sent pictures from those times and put me in touch with other Old Boys.

I am not only indebted to, but am in awe of my talented colleagues in what was then known as CIA's Technical Services Division, and to the man who led us – the late Dr. Sidney Gottlieb. He had a carving on his desk of a turtle. Its legend read: *"Behold the Turtle – It never advances unless it sticks its neck out."* It was the creed by which we lived.

Lastly, I thank (or blame it all on) Mrs. Anne Hayden, whose discovery of a photograph from 1937 launched me on this project in the first place.

***

I

Germany: 1928 – 1937

"When it rains, it rains alike, upon the Just and Unjust fellers, but more upon the Just, because, the Unjust steal the Just's umbrellas." It is one of those Profound Truths little boys are inclined to quote, at the onset of puberty, to display their erudition.

But Just or Unjust, life's rains mostly passed me by, and I rarely needed an umbrella. I was born white; I was born healthy and my family was very well off. I was born in Germany, just as Hitler was coming to power, and I was born a Jew. Which maybe wasn't all that fortunate, but I was born in Hamburg – one of the Hanseatic League cities which, for longer than many German municipalities, resisted domination by the Nazis.

My mother was a Formidable American. She detested all things German, criticized Adolph Hitler constantly and was convinced *der Fuehrer* would not dare to step on an American woman's toes. More likely, Hitler's Minister of Economics, Dr. Hjalmar Schacht, needed all of the foreign exchange he could get to finance the military[2]; exports were a principal source of such foreign exchange; my dad's firm was one of Germany's most successful exporters, and long after the persecution of other Jews began, we were left alone.

I was far too young to understand the cataclysmic events that were taking shape, but reading about them retrospectively, I can recognize many of the waypoints: I remember how the jack-booted, brown-shirted Nazis would throw us schoolboys a snappy 'Heil Hitler' salute, and how our chests would swell with pride as we returned it. I remember how excited we were in 1934, when we were to be taken up in a zeppelin to bomb Hamburg with leaflets urging a YES vote for Hitler. My parents wouldn't let me go but Hitler won anyway – reportedly with 90% of the vote – and it was that Referendum that cemented his power.

I remember the thrill we felt when *der Fuehrer* reclaimed Helgoland – a tiny but strategically placed island in the North Sea, and later when he re-occupied the Ruhr valley, Germany's industrial heart that had been cut out by the Treaty of Versailles. The British, French and Russians did nothing to stop him.

My father began as an enthusiastic supporter of Hitler. "He's just what Germany needs," he assured my mother, who wanted to move the family to New York. "He has the strength and the discipline to pull this nation out of its doldrums, and restore its honor."

"Honor? What honor," my mother demanded? "They started the war, and they lost it. End of story."

When Hitler's anti-Semitism became more apparent, my father's admiration for Hitler waned, but his loyalty to the Fatherland never flagged. "You will see," he assured her once again, "when this upstart has served his purpose, the sensible German people will get rid of him." But my mother was not convinced.

"I really want to return to the States," she told him. "I can only see this situation getting worse."

The firm of B. Luria & Co., occupied two floors of a large office building overlooking the Alster, an artificial lake with an average depth of only 7'. It had been built for flood control almost 800 years earlier. As the settlement grew, first into a village, then into a town and finally into Germany's largest seaport, commerce clustered on its northern banks, closest to the harbor, while the residential areas spread to the south. Starting in the late 19th Century little steamers began to ply between the two.

The city itself is only a few miles from the North Sea's often boisterous winds, but it is also under the residual influences of the Gulf Stream.
The latter makes for a mild climate, most of the year, and the Alster is a
great sailing lake; it was there that I first came to love the sport.

Like most affluent Europeans, we lived modestly – at least by American standards. We lived in an apartment building, on a canal that led to
the Alster. Its basement was a boat house where we kept our canoe.

My parents entertained and traveled a lot, and I was cared for by a
succession of nannies. But children outgrow their nannies, and my mother
hired a young man as a mentor. He was an ideal 'older brother;' he would
challenge me with tasks that were just a little bit beyond my capabilities
– then shake his head mournfully and tell me that I was too young (or too
weak, or too stupid) to complete them.

Talk about a red flag! I would buckle down, put my back into it and
when I succeeded he'd pretend to be flabbergasted. "Unglaublich!" he would
exclaim, rumpling my hair, and would pass on the 'unbelievable achievement' to my mother – from whom I would receive a second dose of praise.
Years later he became my first agent, but the role reversal didn't work very
well.

B. Luria & Co. did a lot of business with South America. Our summer season is the southern hemisphere's winter – the only time of the year
when (before air conditioning) travel in that region was tolerable. Every
summer my father would spend three months making a circuit of his Latin
American clients. The moment he left, we would pack our bags and board
a ship for the United States, to spend two months on my grandparents'
estate, in Lakeville, CT.

Those were halcyon days and cherished times. I had my mother's un-
divided attention, and she was a lively and adventurous travel companion.
Then too, because B. Luria & Co. shipped so many goods on the major
steamship lines, we received a lot of special favors.

One day a note was delivered to our table. "The Captain needs help
in steering the ship," it said, "and Master Carlos' presence on the bridge is
required."

Realizing that the safety of the entire vessel lay in my hands, I hur-
riedly followed the sailor as we climbed ever higher and arrived on the
bridge. They had placed a box by the binnacle for me to stand on and

stressed the importance of keeping the compass needle squarely centered on the large W. The vessel was on autopilot, of course, but I didn't know from autopilots, and as I spun the great wheel from left to right, the compass needle never wavered.

I reached over to that big, brass gizmo that said Full Ahead and Full Astern, but a sailor quickly intercepted me. "It's broken," he assured me; "we just keep it around for decoration."

"But how do you get the boat to go backwards," I asked? After all, I wasn't born yesterday.

"We talk to the engine room through those speaking tubes." When I reached for a tube he gently took it out of my hand.

"There's nobody in the engine room right now; they are all having lunch."

Sometimes we would interrupt our trips by disembarking at Le Havre to spend a week in Paris, or at Southampton, to visit an old friend, Sir George Lloyd-Jacob. A former RAF ace, he had refused to let doctors amputate a badly wounded limb, and with his crippled left arm encased in a leather sleeve, he cut a dashing figure. By then a judge on Britain's King's court, Sir George had been knighted, and several years later helped my parents get some of their assets out of Germany.

My grandparents lived in New York City, but had a summer home in Lakeville, CT. It was the gathering place for our extended family. Aunts, cousins, children and grandchildren arrived throughout the summer, stayed for a week or two and departed. And every weekend scandalous Cousin Eddy would arrive in his dashing, cream-colored convertible, accompanied by his latest confection. Eyebrows would waggle disapprovingly, and the children would be sent out of the room while sleeping arrangements were discussed:

In 1936, my younger brother David was born. To get me out of the way, my parents put me aboard the Holland-America Line's *SS Rotterdam* and sent me to the United States. Officially, I was under the care of an elderly lady – a Mrs. Gulda, I believe -- but it was a rough crossing and she spent the voyage confined to her cabin.

I had by that time crossed the Atlantic more than a dozen times, in all kinds of weather, and had long since gotten my sea legs. This was a particularly rough crossing, however and barriers (called 'fiddles') had to be raised on all of the tables to keep the dishes from sliding off. On deck, the passengers were either groaning in their deck chairs, or hanging over the leeward rail, communicating with the Atlantic.

But not I. I came up on deck, rubbed my hands together with great satisfaction, smiled genially upon the halt & the lame and remarked enthusiastically on the beauties of the day. One terminally ill passenger was overheard to say: "I just hope I recover enough to throw that little bastard overboard." When I asked the aunts in Lakeville what 'bastards' were, it set the eyebrows to waggling again.

Like most trans-Atlantic liners, the *Rotterdam* put on an exceptionally festive dinner two nights before arrival, with ice sculptures and lavish entertainment. Called the Captain's Dinner, it was a gala affair, with paper hats and noisemakers and confetti heaped on all the tables.

My allocation of confetti was soon used up, but like most 8 year old boys, my pockets were crammed with old candy wrappers and similar junk. I fished them out, tore them up and continued to party. Unfortunately, among the papers I destroyed were my passport and visa. When Immigrations came aboard the following morning, I had no papers. The thoroughly dehydrated Mrs. Gulda was of little help – perhaps they wouldn't accept her word because she was not a blood relative -- and I was taken off the ship to Ellis Island, where my grandmother had to claim me. It took most of the day to straighten things out. Eyebrows waggled disapprovingly, big time.

But the halcyon days were coming to an end, and in Germany there was a palpable change in the climate. Nationalistic fervor was busting out all over. As mentioned, Hitler had boldly reclaimed the Rhineland, and no one had tried to stop him. That August, Germany hosted a triumphant Olympic Games, winning 89 Gold medals vs. 56 for the US, and her boxing champion, Max Schmeling, defeated America's Brown Bomber, Joe Louis. That *clearly* proved the superiority of the Aryan races. Unfortunately Jesse Owens, a black sharecropper's son, won four Gold Medals and left Germany's track team in the dust, and a year later in a rematch, Joe Louis, beat Max Schmeling in 2 minutes, 10 seconds of the first round. However, 'good' Germans were quickly persuaded that there must have been foul play – no doubt organized by the Jews.

I had been attending the Lehman Schule, run by two Jewish spinsters, but it had been closed; I was transferred to the safely-Lutheran, Bertram Schule, where we sang Hitler's praises every morning in our underwear and engaged in vigorous calisthenics. *Kraft Durch Freude (Strength through Joy)* -- or maybe it was the other way around. My closest friend, Wolfgang Mueller, began to avoid me; his father was a functionary in the Nazi Party, and when I stopped by his house one day, the maid told me he was out. I could hear him plainly, playing and laughing with his friends, and I began to push my way past the housekeeper. *"Er ist nicht zu Hause!"* she repeated, grabbed me firmly by the shoulder and shoved me out the door. I was also not allowed to sign up again for the riding academy.

The Nuremberg Declaration, stripping Jews of their German citizenship, had been passed the year before, and while its implementation in Hamburg had been delayed because of that city's special status, the handwriting was on the wall.

"I'm taking the children to the States," my mother announced, early in 1937. "I hope you come, too, but I'm going to take them just as soon as the baby is old enough to travel."

With great reluctance, my father agreed, and planning for our exodus began. It would in fact take almost two years to make the arrangements and to surreptitiously transfer many of their assets to the United States, but a first step was to get me out of the country. During the 1937 Christmas break, I was enrolled in a British boarding school, and whisked off to Kent.

✡✡✡

2

TORMORE SCHOOL: 1938 –1939

"No." I wailed, struggling to break free, "No. I don't want to stay here. Why can't we just go home?"

My mother had me firmly by the wrist, half dragging me toward the school. It was Saturday, January 15th, 1938, and school would be resuming the following week. We had left Hamburg right after Christmas and spent a fortnight in London, buying the uniforms and other supplies the school required, then had taken the Southern Railroad to the little town of Upper Deal, Kent -- right on the Dover Coast. A cold winter rain swept off the Channel, and my mother wrestled unsuccessfully with an umbrella while trying to keep me from breaking free. The icy rain seeped down my collar as she steered us toward a nearby tearoom.

"You may not be old enough to understand *why* it is happening, but you certainly have seen *what* is happening," she told me for the hundredth time. "Those horrid signs on more and more shop windows: *"Juden 'Rauss"* (Jews, Get Out.), and *"Hier Werden Juden Nicht Bedient."* (This establishment will not serve Jews) More and more of your friends won't play with you. You were pushed out of the riding academy, and it is just going to get worse."

"But we're not *Jewish,* I wailed again. We celebrate Christmas and Easter; I go to a Lutheran school; I've never even set *foot* in a synagogue."

"Officially, we're Jewish," she said flatly. "Look at your passport; it has a big 'J' stamped on it. It hasn't happened in Hamburg, yet, but throughout much of Germany, the Jews have had to sew a large, yellow Star of David on their clothing. The Nazis won't touch me, because I'm an American, and for the moment they are leaving your father alone, but you are not safe, and we have to get you out.

"We're going to move to New York, as soon as we can arrange it," she continued, but until then I have to go back to Hamburg, and you are going to have to stay here. I'll be visiting you often, though" she added; "I promise you that."

Somewhat mollified I let her lead me into the school – and almost threw up. Grim is the only way to describe it: dark, chilly hallways, smelling strongly of carbolic acid and floor wax; cracked linoleum floors; row upon row of empty pegs lining the wall, each labeled with the name of a student who would be arriving the following day.

Just the last names, of course, for that is the British way; had there been four Smiths, they would have been called Smith Maximus, Smith

Major, Smith Minor and Smith Minimus, in the order of their ages. I never did find out what -- God forbid. -- a fifth Smith would have been called, or how Smith twins would have been labeled. But that was academic, for the school was a very small one, and the chances of there being a fifth Smith were miniscule. Tormore, you see, was Church of England, and the conventional wisdom was that only Roman Catholics have that many children.

Catholics were not welcome at Tormore -- not because of their allegiance to Rome, but because they had to be served fish on Fridays. Tormore was not about to serve fish on Fridays. Tormore served mutton, creamed leeks and boiled potatoes six days of the week -- maybe because it was more economical to buy in bulk; maybe because it was the only dish that Cook knew how to prepare. Sundays in any event were Cook's day off, and parents were encouraged to take the children elsewhere for dinner; those of us who remained behind were served porridge.

Jews were not welcome at Tormore either, which created a bit of a problem. I would never have been admitted to Tormore, had it not been for some serious arm-twisting by Sir George Lloyd-Jacob.

Sir George was a very good arm-twister: he was a barrister who had gone on to become a World War I fighter pilot, had returned to the bar after the Armistice, and by 1938 had become a judge. He may have been one of my mothers many lovers, and at one point I wondered whether he was perhaps my real father. Because I had been born less than eight months after my mother had married, and really didn't look much like my German father.

Sir George could not have been kinder to me all the time I was at Tormore; he often took me to lunch on Sundays, and comforted me when I was homesick. But ten years later, when I spent two weeks at his home in Surrey and developed a real crush on his daughter, he made it quite clear that the romance would go no further. Was it perhaps that she was really my sister? I don't know -- but I didn't look a bit like Sir George, either.

The Headmaster led us into his study, which was just as cold as the hallways, despite a small wood fire. A rack of canes and switches occupied one corner.

"That's the Discipline Corner," he remarked, fixing me with a baleful stare. Then added, ominously, "I trust you will not spend any time there." His trust was misplaced; I got to know it well.

His wife was in the study as well, and they called in Matron, a beefy, red-faced, no-nonsense woman, straight out of the pages of Dickens; she would give us our weekly baths. The three of them glared at me with unfeigned exasperation, then Matron grudgingly gave us a tour of the school.

Tormore's escutcheon, which also appeared on the breast pocket of our blazers, consisted of a truncated arm, clad in mail, its hand clutching a Crusader's sword.

The school stood on land that had belonged to the Crown – to Henry VIII, I believe - and a large pond occupied a corner of the estate. Legend has it that the Sovereign announced a contest, promising to deed the land to the first knight who could swim across the pond in full mail, and touch the opposite bank. As the contestants neared the finish, one knight -- realizing that he was going to lose -- drew his sword, cut off his left arm and flung it to the shore. He may have bled to death, but he was deeded the land.

Great story, right? But I suspect it is apocryphal, for the escutcheon bears a distinct resemblance to the Coat of Arms of the MacDonald clan, and the Master of the Royal Society of Heraldry wrote in answer to my query that it is not uncommon for schools to adopt the Arms of their founders. A MacDonald had indeed established the school.

Apocryphal or true, the escutcheon certainly symbolized what Tormore stood for and what it drummed into our heads: Courage, Sacrifice, Public Service and – perhaps uncharacteristically for British society of that day -- the importance of thinking outside the box.

The Head's name was Frank Turner, his initials were FGT and his nickname, though never to his face of course, was FIDGET. His wife was Mary O. S. Turner, or MOST. FIDGET and MOST were like two hungry wolves, circling a flock of Shropshire sheep. They were everywhere; had eyes in the backs of their heads, and made sure that no transgression, however slight, went unpunished.

We were housed in dormitories, 12 -14 boys to a room, a chamber pot under each bed, and a long table at the end of the room, with bowls for washing up. No running water, of course; we had to fetch it in large pails from a lower floor.

Just before lights out, FIDGET and MOST would come into the rooms, single out the day's transgressors and have them bend over the foot of their beds. MOST would pull down their pajama bottoms and FIDGET would whack them with a hard-soled slipper. If we whimpered, we were whacked some more. Painful as these slipperings were, they were a cakewalk compared to a visit to the Discipline Corner.

Sounds grim, doesn't it? But in the year and a half I spent there, I really grew to love that school, and FIDGET, shown here, apparently came to like me, too. On the cricket pitch I showed a real knack for bowling, and he coached me tirelessly. I was a good swimmer, too, for I had learned the crawl, while British boys were raised on the stodgy breast stroke.

Unlike their American cousins, the British were slow to make friends -- it took them a long time to navigate the shoals of class, breeding and accent. But once they got past all that, the friendships formed were deep and enduring.

Tormore School was just a mile or two from the Dover coast, and 20 miles or so from France. After Dunkirk, Tormore was moved inland, out of harm's way, and its students were incorporated into a larger school. It resumed operations after the war, but according to a schoolmate with whom I corresponded, it burned down in the mid-1980's. Today the land serves as a park named the Tormore Park. At its entrance stands a bas relief -- of a truncated arm, clad in mail; its hand clutching a sword.

As she had promised, my mother visited me every couple of months – though not solely out of maternal concern. She was extremely flat-chested, and while that may have been an asset in the flapper era, it was definitely not the fashion in the thirties. She had a series of padded bras made that also contained cleverly concealed pockets, and on every visit to England she smuggled out gold coins and precious jewels, leaving them with Sir George for safekeeping. When they finally emigrated, my parents knew that they would not be allowed to leave Germany with more than the clothes on their back, and they wanted to get as many of their assets as possible out of the country.

Meanwhile, my dad developed various schemes to shift some of B. Luria & Co.'s assets out of Germany. Among other things, his firm absorbed the cost of goods purchased by his foreign customers, while they in turn paid for such goods by deposits to a New York bank. He knew the deception would be discovered when the books were audited, but he expected to be long gone by that time, and while he was in effect stealing from the firm, he was its sole owner, and its assets would be appropriated by the Nazis when he emigrated.

My parents and my brother David moved permanently to the United States in December of 1938, while I remained in the British school. I followed when the academic year ended, shortly before the war started in 1939, and when I left I think I wailed as long and as loudly as I had when I arrived. Well, perhaps not quite as long, for I got to cross on the *SS Washington* all by myself -- an 11 year old boy who had by then acquired a charming British accent, who was taken under every matronly wing, who was spoiled rotten by the crew — and who took *very* good care of his passport.

Typically, ocean liners reach New York very early in the morning, and approach a city that is just coming awake. Dawn colors the sky a delicate mauve and garlands of lights stretch across the bridges like ragged strings of pearls.

Aboard, a whole kaleidoscope of raw emotions: immigrants apprehensive about their new lives; tourists excited about their forthcoming adventures, and ex-pats and weary world travelers, just glad to get home.

But it is the passage past the Statue of Liberty that is the most awe inspiring and brings a lump to the throat. This was my eighth, west-bound crossing and it was always the same: passengers crowded the port rail, overwhelmed with emotion as the vessel glided past that magnificent statue. A thousand souls aboard, and the only sounds those of the ship's bow as it sliced gently through the water. The Lady's torch had not yet been extinguished; the harbor was mirror-smooth and the sun was just starting to touch the tops of the towering buildings:

Awake, for Morning, as the scourge of night,
Has cast the stone that puts the stars to flight.
And lo, the Hunter of the East has caught
The Sultan's towers in a noose of light...

...And as the cock crowed, those who stood before
The portals shouted: "Open now the door!
You know how little time we have to stay,
And once departed, may return no more[3]

Pier 57 North River, then the United States Lines' premier facility, was barely wide enough to accommodate the *SS Washington*, and warping her into her berth was no mean operation. But much of our extended family was on the pier to greet me, my mother waving frantically and crying, and even my stern and dour father brushing away a surreptitious tear. We were together, now; all of us, and in America. A whole new life was beginning.

***

3

THE CIA YEARS

Prologue:

This chapter is in part a personal memoir, in part a history of a lesser-known aspect of the Cold War, and in part a polemic.

What qualifies me to write such a monograph? That's simple: very little. I was merely one of a number of mid-level managers; I was neither a member of the inner councils, nor did I serve on the policy-making levels of CIA. But for a period I occupied an unusual vantage point. I was the Executive Officer (or EXO) of an organization that developed and deployed intelligence collection systems in denied areas, and that created devices to assist human sources – the classic spies. It provided me with an understanding of the science and engineering that CIA was exploiting, a deep respect for the imagination and competence of the engineers and technicians who developed and deployed these devices, and an intimate look at the courage and resourcefulness of many of CIA's quite extraordinary agents.

I served during the era in which technology rose to prominence, became the fair-haired child of the Intelligence Community and increasingly muscled human source intelligence aside. I cite numerous cases as examples, and my daughter Sarah, the American Literature professor, quite properly asked why I wanted to reprise so many cases that had been written about before? Precisely because it is the *sum* of their successes that explains why we were seduced by technology and funneled fewer and fewer resources into the recruitment of human sources.

It was an evolution that had merit when we were confronting nation-states, with defined borders and fixed targets, but one that displayed its shortcomings on 9/11. Terrorist cells have no borders, no capitals, no airfields or missile silos and few fixed locations. Many of our collection systems were rendered useless, and by then we had too few officers with the experience, area knowledge and requisite language skills to recruit human sources.

The polemic that appears at the end of this chapter was prompted by the wave of criticism that engulfed the Intelligence Community in general (and CIA in particular) after 9/11, The Senate's Select Committee on Intelligence, the 9/11 Commission, the Bush Administration and the media were quick to identify the Community's shortcomings, and many of their criticisms were assuredly justified. But never once was the 3,000 lb elephant in the room mentioned: the role that public pressure played in the erosion of America's Intelligence capability.

With other programs clamoring for funds from perpetually strained Federal budgets, both Presidents Clinton and Bush severely cut allocations to the Intelligence Community, and prior to 9/11, the latter displayed only a cursory interest in Intelligence products. For specialists whose area knowledge and language skills were much in demand both by universities, multi-national corporations and think tanks, there was little incentive to remain; they left in droves, and throughout the 1990's that exodus stripped CIA of many of its best and its brightest.

It was neither the first time, nor would it be the last that America savaged its Intelligence capabilities to save money, but on 9/11 we once again learned a hard truth: *"If you think Intelligence is expensive, try Ignorance."*

***

I

The Clandestine Service:

October, 1950. The Korean War was in full swing and upon graduation my draft deferment would expire. When the Army Recruiter came on campus, I asked him about the possibility of enlisting and choosing my branch of the service. What specialty? Well, Intelligence had a nice ring to it – cerebral rather than physical, most of the work was indoors, and if one could believe the novels, some of it even in the bedroom.

I pointed out that I had been born and raised in Germany (neglecting to mention that I had forgotten much of the language), exaggerated my area knowledge, stressed that my Dad had been a prominent exporter in Hamburg, and stated that I myself had spent two years working for an import/export firm – after having been ignominiously thrown out of Swarthmore College. Only after maturing a bit did I complete my degree.

He was interested. I had amassed a good (if belated) academic record, and I was willing to sign up for the minimum four years. But then he asked:

"When did you become a naturalized citizen?"

"1944"

"Sorry, G2 requires a minimum of ten years as a citizen for a Top Secret clearance."

What the hell, Navy's got better food anyway, so I went around to the Navy recruiter:

"Sorry, ONI requires a minimum of fifteen years as a citizen for a Top Secret clearance."

I returned to school, resigned to the idea that I would be drafted the following May. Shortly after Thanksgiving, however, a little man knocked on the door of the house where I was living, flashed some credentials that I didn't look at too closely, and said he wanted to talk.

"I've heard that you were born and raised in Germany."

"Yes, that's right. Who told you that?"

"And that your father was a prominent exporter?"

"Yes – but who told you that?"

"I'm not at liberty to say; just answer the questions. You majored in Economics and minored in Marketing?"

"That's right."

"And intend to make the import/export field your career?"

"You've been talking to the Army recruiter, right?"

"Just answer the questions, please, or this interview is over. And you believe that you could make a contribution to the Intelligence field?"

"Yes. But perhaps you have also 'heard' that I haven't been a citizen long enough to qualify."

"In fact, I have. But my people don't care about that."

"Your people? Who are 'your people' anyway? Let me see your credentials again."

His impressive looking badge said that be represented the CIA – which few people had heard of in 1950 He said that it was the follow-on to the military's OSS, which had been disbanded after WW-II. He said that the 'Agency' (as he called it) was interested in people with my qualifications.

"Doing what?"

"I'm not at liberty to say. But it would satisfy your military service requirements."

Clearly we were now entering what is known as the 'negotiation phase,' and I wasn't about to agree without some haggling.

"I'll need time to think about this."

He told me to take as much time as I needed. I screwed my face into a grimace of intense concentration, and stroked my beardless chin reflectively. Forty five seconds seemed about right, and I agreed.

We took shelter in a restaurant, and he waited while I filled out a fairly lengthy application. He looked it over carefully, asked some additional questions for clarification and finally seemed satisfied.

"If my people are interested, you will receive a letter postmarked Cleveland." He displayed a phone number. "You will then call this number, introduce yourself as Alex, and further instructions will be provided."

Man, this was really heads-up stuff! I started to write down the phone number, but he said I had to memorize it.

Of course the moment he left, I wrote down the number, and in late February the letter from Cleveland arrived: my marching orders. I squeezed into a phone booth and dialed the number I had been given. A woman answered.

"This is Alex," I whispered, conspiratorially.

"Who? Speak up, please; I can't hear you."

"Alex," I repeated. "This is *Alex*."

"Alex who," the woman asked?

"Lady," I said, becoming agitated – Korea was looming menacingly on the horizon – "I was told to call this number and say that my name is 'Alex' – which it isn't – and that I would be given further instructions – which I haven't been. Apparently that's the way you people *do* things."

There was a long silence while she digested this bit of intelligence, then she asked, sweetly,

"And what number were you supposed to call?"

So I had reversed a couple of digits. It happens. Get over it!

On the second attempt, however, I got it right, and when I had been patched through to the right party, I found myself speaking to a man with a distinct German accent.

"As a New Yorker," he said, after the preliminaries; "you probably know the Commodore Hotel."

"Next to Grand Central Station? Sure."

"There's a big clock at the entrance. I will meet you there at 11:00 AM on Saturday. I'll be wearing a gray overcoat, a gray fedora with a small black feather, and I will be carrying a copy of the *Economist* under my left arm; the masthead will be clearly visible. You will come up to me and ask me for directions to the Madison Avenue subway."

"There isn't any Madison Avenue subway," I offered, helpfully.

He sighed audibly at my naïveté: "Exactly."

We met as planned, and he took me to lunch at a small restaurant. He said his name was Fred. He appeared to be about 30, had closely cropped black hair and a compact, muscular build; he looked vaguely familiar.

He explained that after the war, the government had closed down its primary intelligence service – the OSS -- and disbanded its assets. Now, with the growing threat from the USSR, it had to start again -- almost from scratch. A few of the old-timers, himself included, had rejoined, but CIA was embarked upon a major expansion.

He suddenly switched to German, and we chatted about Hamburg. He knew it well. Very well. In fact, he had attended my primary school, the Lehman Schule, some eight years ahead of me, and his family had been friendly with the two sisters who ran the place. Then he really blew my mind: "My twin brothers," he said, "were three years ahead of you, at George School."

"Oh my God -- Hans and Rudi. Of course. No wonder you looked familiar. Are they working for your .. er, 'organization' as well?"

"The Company," he said. "We call it the Company."

His proposition was tempting: "I don't know if I can bring it off, but I'd like to get you back to Hamburg -- to follow in your father's footsteps. It would be a logical move, after all: one that fits with your academic background and with your career plans.

"Your father's old firm -- or what is left of it -- still exists, and it would be the ideal place for you to serve an apprenticeship and to re-establish relations with many of your father's former clients. When you then return to New York, your experience and your contacts will make you very marketable in foreign trade circles. Your credentials, in fact, will be impeccable and hard to beat. Furthermore, in addition to what you might earn from your cover job, we will be paying you a salary."

"That's great, Fred, but I can't just leave the country: I've already been ordered to report for my pre-induction physical."

"We can take care of that."

"But you must have dozens of employees more experienced than I who could do the job."

"Very candidly, Carlos, for a career officer it would be a bullshit assignment. He's out there, at the end of a string, known to only to a handful of people. To the honchos at Headquarters he is a faceless cryptonym, and when selections are being made for management positions and advancement, no one of influence knows him. But for someone like you, who does not intend to make a career of CIA, it's an ideal posting; it will leave you with good commercial experience, as well as a substantial nest-egg."

"I guess I've never thought of Hamburg as a center of the Cold War."

"Communism had its roots in the maritime trades," Fred explained. "It grew legs in Russia's Merchant Marine service, and spread rapidly through the old Hanseatic League networks: Danzig, Luebeck, Hamburg, Rotterdam, Antwerp, Cherbourg, etc. In our own port cities, the International Longshoreman's Unions is riddled with communist activity, and in each of these centers Soviet intelligence officers are busily at work, gathering information, and recruiting new sources.

"In Hamburg, your task would be to identify and develop some of these Soviet Intel officers, so that we could target them for recruitment."

"You want me to recruit spies for you?"

"No," he said sharply, "you're not listening. If you tried to recruit a Soviet and failed, your cover would be blown, and your usefulness to us would be over. We would just want you to identify them, and get to know them.

"We need to know as much as possible about them, about their families, about their needs, about their hopes and aspirations — about what drives them. A posting to the West is a plum for a Soviet: few shortages, comfortable housing, a permissive society. It provides him countless opportunities to engage in black market and other shady activities, to feather his nest and to satisfy his appetites. He will go to great lengths to keep such an assignment."

"I'm getting married in the fall. Would my wife stay behind, in Washington?"

"No, she would accompany you. But she will need a security clearance, and if for any reason she can't be cleared, the deal's off; it's as simple as that."

"Fred, my father is gonna blow a gasket when he hears about this – and there's no way of keeping it from him. I wouldn't know how to approach him."

"That's easy – you don't. If this project materializes, (and at this point that's still a very big 'if'), a senior government official will invite him to Washington, will lay out the plan in broad strokes and ask for his cooperation. As a patriotic American, recently naturalized, I don't think he'll turn down such a request from his government, do you? But if he does, that's the end of it."

It sounded exciting. And reasonable, too. In fact, I knew where I would start: with Gunther, the young man my parents had hired as an 'older brother, and whose parents had had strong Socialist leanings. In 1938 he had joined the Merchant Marine and had gotten his ticket as a 3rd officer aboard a tramp steamer that shuttled between the North Sea ports and the Aegean. He had remained there until he had been drafted into the *Kriegsmarine* and had been assigned to Harbor Patrol. Perhaps he still had contacts in what remained of the maritime service.

"I'm going to Europe after graduation," I told Fred, excitedly. "Maybe I can recruit him to help me, for I'll be spending a week in Hamburg."

"No, that is exactly what you must *not* do," Fred replied, testily, "for the reasons I just explained. Suppose he turns you down? Worse, suppose he turns you *in.* Your entire value to us would be lost. Look him up; catch up on old times; try to determine where his political sympathies lie, but do not even hint at any kind of clandestine activity. Then we'll talk further when you get back."

When I returned to Hamburg that summer, vast stretches of the city still lay in ruins. The industrial center had been completely flattened, but the harbor was being cleared and the docks were being rebuilt.

Little of the once-graceful St. Nikkolai church was still standing, and to this day its ruins remain as a memorial to the city's destruction. Erected in the first half of the 19th Century, it celebrated Bismarck's consolidation of the German empire, Kaiser Wilhelm's boisterous saber-rattling and the Nazi's attempts to conquer the world. Now its broken steeple reached vainly for the skies, its shattered windows stared blindly down upon a city that it could no longer see, and a devastation it could not possibly comprehend. A brass plaque, embedded in its remains said simply: "Forgive us, Lord; this madness we brought upon ourselves."

St. Pauli's Reeperbahn, however, the city's famous red light district, was back in full swing. Sturdy steel walls, with openings just wide enough for one pedestrian to pass through at a time, still blocked the streets, where nearly naked girls sat in their picture windows, enticing passersby to stop in for a romp, and where a few American cigarettes, or 100 gms. of coffee were the currencies of choice.

The war and the years of hardship that followed had taken their toll on Gunther. He was distraught, directionless and struggling to survive. His parents had been killed in the July 27th, 1943 fire-bombing that had snuffed out 40,000 lives in a single night. Gunther was hoping to go back to sea, but there were thousands of experienced and unemployed sailors looking for jobs, and the competition was fierce.

He said that in 1939 he had briefly flirted with joining the KPD, the German Communist Party, because it was the only organized force against Nazism. But he didn't do so. By then the Party had been so thoroughly penetrated by the Gestapo that it would have been suicidal. Then, talks with German POWs who had returned from the East and the brutality of the Russian occupation of the Soviet Zone had turned him against the Russian brand of communism. Perhaps he was telling me all this because anti-communist fervor in the United States had reached a fever pitch, but I didn't think so.

Martha and I had announced our engagement shortly before I had gone abroad. She knew nothing about my conversation with Fred and when I returned from Europe in mid-July, she broke off our engagement. She didn't like New York and didn't relish the prospect of living there. She and my mother didn't like one another and that would just make life more difficult It. And both she and her parents were concerned that I was frittering away a summer in Europe, instead of looking for a job.

I was devastated. A basket case, and probably would have remained so for many months. But there was also a message from Fred, asking me to call. He confirmed that I had been hired, and ordered me to Washington. It would put me that much closer to Martha. It would give me another chance.

I formally began working for the Agency in August of 1951 – ostensibly as one of a group of researcher/translators for a historical division, housed in rented office space near Union Station. We were dispatched from there to various archival centers around town, to wade through captured WW-II documents, to catalogue them and to comb them for bits of significant data.

But I headed instead for a safehouse on M street for tutorial training in what was called 'tradecrafts.' I arrived at around 8:45, put on the coffee and awaited the instructors who shuttled in to train me in the esoteric skills of intelligence. Between sessions I listened to *Deutsche Welle*, Germany's equivalent of *Voice of America*, and ploughed my way through *Der Spiegel*, roughly comparable to *Time Magazine*. From time to time I was sent out to practice making or servicing dead drops – hiding things like a 35mm film canister behind a loose brick, or recovering a message.

The need for thoroughness ran as a central thread through all of the training and came right from the top – from Alan Dulles, the Director of Central Intelligence. In his book, *The Craft of Intelligence*, he reflects on an incident in 1917: When America entered the first World War, Mr. Dulles was a young Foreign Service officer, stationed in Bern. It was a Sunday, he was the designated Duty Officer and the switchboard called to say that there was a Russian national who had something very important to discuss with the American ambassador.

There had been a succession of such calls from assorted cranks and anarchists all summer long, and as Duty Officer it was Mr. Dulles' responsibility to interview such people before bothering the Ambassador. But Mr. Dulles had a tennis date with a pretty lady he had been pursuing for months. He asked the switchboard to remind the caller that it was Sunday, that the Embassy was closed, and that it would reopen early the next morning.

Vladimir Illitsch Lenin, however, could not wait. He was on his way back to Russia. He had a train to catch, and a revolution to launch that would hold the world hostage for the next seventy-two years.

Twice I sent Martha flowers — signing the card 'from an unknown admirer.' I visited the Corcoran, where her best friend staffed the Information Desk, and made sure that I was spotted. "I'm almost certain I saw Carlos this afternoon," Dianne reported to Martha. "Have you heard from him?" During my field exercises I would try to eat lunch at a small restaurant on Connecticut Avenue, near the National Child Research Center, where Martha worked, and one day I ran into her.

"Carlos. How long have you been here," she wanted to know? "Dee thought she had seen you at the Corcoran."

"About a month."

"And what are you doing here; are you working?"

"Sort of," I confided, hoping that a dash of mystery might pique her curiosity. She didn't bite. "I'm not supposed to talk about it," I added, for good measure.

"Well, you might have called me," she said, petulantly.

"I wanted to, but they're going to send me abroad soon. And it may be *dangerous*."

Nothing! Still no reaction; she wasn't the least bit curious about who 'they' were, or where I might be sent. "That's why I sent those flowers -- anonymously," I added, a little desperately, really pushing my luck.

Martha looked at me for a long time: "Well," she said, at last: "that was very sweet. And I have missed you."

One day, as an exercise, I was instructed to recover an ostensible 'packet of money,' taped to the underside of a toilet's water tank, in the third stall of the Library of Congress' men's room. When I arrived, the stall was occupied. I returned ten minutes later and the stall was still occupied -- or was now being used by someone else. And yet again, ten minutes after that. In fact all of the stalls were now in use, with a line of men awaiting their turn.

I could come back later, but suppose a janitor found the packet when cleaning the rest room? I decided to wait, and as my turn came up, I let others go ahead of me, hoping vainly for stall #3 to be vacated.

Suddenly two burly Security men barged into the men's room, grabbed me by the arms, shoved me up against the wall and escorted me out in handcuffs. I was charged with loitering for lewd and lascivious purposes.

They gave me a hard time, but they hadn't any proof; no one had ac-
cused me of accosting them. I explained that I needed to be near a toilet, for
I had taken a strong laxative that morning and when it worked, I wouldn't
have much advance warning. Pretty weak – but it was the best I could come
up with on short notice. They didn't believe it, but after what seemed like
an hour (and was probably closer to ten minutes), they let me go.

Figuring that there would have been a shift change by 8:00 PM and
that a different security crew would be in place, I returned just before the
library closed for the night and retrieved the package.

Fred came by from time to time to check on my progress, to bring me
copies of Hamburg's newspaper, *Die Welt*, and to critique my performance.
The restroom incident, he told me, had been a set-up. A test. He gave the
laxative story a C, but scolded me for having decided to hang around at
all.

"Money," he said, sternly, "can always be replaced, but it takes years to
prepare and infiltrate an agent." Then he really jumped on me for having
returned that night:

"If the security folks had been in the least bit suspicious of your
story," he said, "they would have staked out that restroom and would have
arrested you the moment you showed up again.

"That's what we should have done," he added ruefully, "only we didn't
think you'd be that stupid."

Among the many lessons *not* learned at mother's knee is lock-picking
– a skill that every spy worthy of the name is supposed to master. Leo was
my instructor and he tore out more and more of his few remaining hairs as
he tried to teach me the proper manipulation of assorted picks and tension
bars. Patience triumphed, however, and eventually I was ready for the final
exam – a mock-up containing a variety of luggage locks, padlocks, door
locks and a safe door with an impressive looking combination lock. I got
through the latter almost at once, because unbeknownst to Leo, I had done
a little homework of my own: a fellow instructor had given me Leo's and
his wife's birthdays, and it was the latter that did the trick. Nine times out
of ten, people will use their street address, a portion of their phone number
or a birthday, etc., to set a combination lock. Probably half of the Nazis set
their combination locks to 20-04-89 – Adolf Hitler's birthday.

Trying hard to suppress a smirk, I tackled the last challenge – a formidable looking dead bolt mounted in an 8" x 12" hinged door section, set in a fixed door frame. I was allowed 5 minutes, but even with an extra three, I couldn't open it.

With a profound sigh, Leo reached across my shoulder, turned the door knob, and pushed. The door swung open; it had not been locked at all!

So much for the smirk.

An instructor named Rupert came to the safehouse regularly to coach me in the detection and avoidance of surveillance. I would be sent out on one task or another, would try to spot the "hostiles," as we termed them, and would have to decide whether to abort or to carry out the task. Better safe than sorry, of course, but the safe course meant that the task did not get done. Sometimes there would be no hostiles at all, but I'd 'see them' nonetheless; at other times I'd miss them entirely, and they'd nail me. But with practice I slowly improved, and finally Rupert was satisfied.

Heady stuff, and for the most part I loved it. But there was one small problem that Fred had not anticipated: Following WW-II, the defeated Germany was divided into four zones: British, French, Soviet and American. My destination was in the British zone. Midway in my training, Fred fired off a courtesy message to the British to tell them that CIA would be sending an officer to work in their zone. "Frightfully decent of you chaps," the Brits replied, "but we believe we can manage quite nicely without your help." And thus ended the Hamburg assignment.

Within a few weeks, however, an official cover position opened up in Germany, and the Desk nominated me to Frankfurt, stressing that I had language fluency.

"Yeah, right." the Station replied. "You've sent a lot of people over here, claiming they speak fluent German, and they can't even ask directions to the toilet. We want this man tested."

Fred came to the rescue. He expanded upon my background, allowed that I had emigrated at the age of 10 and hadn't spoken the language since, but stressed that I had listened to German broadcasts and read German newspapers during my training. He went on at some length, for brevity was not Fred's strong suit.

All CIA cable traffic had to be encrypted, however, and in the early 50's, long before the advent of computers, such encryption was done by hand. It cost $1 per character (we were told) to encrypt a message, and Fred's supervisor slashed his cable to the bone. The message that finally made its way to the transmission center, said simply:

"Subject has the vocabulary of a 10 year old."

And the base replied, resignedly, "We'll take him."

Persistence and dogged determination paid off, and Martha again agreed to marry me, but with our departure for Frankfurt now scheduled for early February, time was short. Invitations went out a week before Christmas, announcing a wedding date of January 5th, and in the protocol-conscious Washington of the 1950's, such unseemly haste could mean only one thing: the bride was already pregnant; a quick departure for Germany would conveniently mask the baby's birth. In fact, Martha wasn't pregnant, and the baby wasn't born for another two years — but such corrections rarely make the front page.

Back at Headquarters, Fred continued to smart over the Brits' rejection of his proposal to send a CIA officer to their zone. Why was it so summarily dismissed? CIA and MI-6 had a tradition of working very closely together. He hadn't thought that he needed to get the Brits concurrence at all, and had in fact notified them merely as a courtesy. But they had slammed the door in his face.

Only years later did I come across a possible explanation: In 1952, MI-6's Hamburg Station Chief was a man named George Blake, later unmasked as a top-level Soviet penetration of Britain's Secret Service; perhaps he didn't want a CIA type nosing around in his cabbage patch.

Fred had pursued the lead I had given him, vetted Gunther and on a trip to Hamburg had recruited him. In part because I knew him, but probably even more because Fred didn't think he'd be all that productive a source, they assigned him to me — a brand new and very green case officer.

Gunther was told to be at the Renzelstrasse entrance to the city's botanical garden at a designated time on a particular Tuesday. As a recognition signal, he was told, a man would ask him for directions to a particular restaurant, just a few blocks to the East

I traveled to Hamburg from Frankfurt, two days in advance of the scheduled meeting, registered at a small, unobtrusive pension near the train station, and spent the time exploring and reacquainting myself with the city. On the designated Tuesday, I arrived at the meeting site an hour early.

Trolley tracks ran down the center of the street and a restaurant, across from the park's entrance had an outdoor deck, shaded by a large awning. I settled down at a secluded table to see whether Gunther would come alone or would arrive escorted.

But there was no unusual activity as the hour approached, and he seemed to be alone when he stepped off the trolley. From the recesses of the restaurant I watched him as he paced back and forth, occasionally looking at his watch, but making no effort to communicate with or signal anyone else. Finally, he concluded that no one was going to show up and joined the queue waiting at the trolley stop for the next tram to arrive.

I had already paid my bill, and as the tram clanged its warning bell, walked briskly from the restaurant, joined the end of the queue, and hopped on board at the last moment. I worked my way through the crowded trolley until I was standing directly behind him. I mumbled the recognition signal, then told him: "Don't turn around. Just get off at the next stop and walk North; I'll catch up with you."

I continued pushing my way through the crowd until I was near the exit. As the trolley slowed, I hopped off and headed South, turned after a half block and retraced my steps. It put me about 100 meters behind him, and gave me another chance to see whether he was being shadowed by a hostile, or escorted by a protective surveillance. After two or three blocks I caught up with him and we turned into a small café for our first substantive meeting.

Gunther was neither surprised nor particularly pleased to see me. In his recruitment pitch, Fred had revealed facts that he could only have learned from me, and Gunther felt that I had callously capitalized on a past friendship. He had agreed to Fred's pitch only because of the reports coming out of the East, following the Soviet's repression of the June uprising in East Berlin, and the stories being told of Soviet brutality by POWs returning from the USSR. A close friend of his, an anti-communist journalist, had been kidnapped in broad daylight by the Soviets and had not been heard from since, and the economic resurgence in the Allied-controlled portions of Germany was clearly greater than that in the East.

He resented my duplicity, however, and my inexperience in motivating a source became very obvious. When I talked about America's altruism as evidenced by the Marshall Plan, he asked whether it would have been implemented had it not been for the Soviet threat? When I spoke of our deep respect for human life, he countered with Nagasaki and Hiroshima. When I quoted Learned Hand that the true spirit of liberty is never being absolutely certain that you are right, and always being open to dissenting views, he came back at me with Joe McCarthy's witch hunts, and his two henchmen, Cohen & Shine, who were at that moment, touring Europe and making a mockery of the democratic process.

"If America 'wins' the Cold War," he asked, "what makes you think she won't abuse her power just as victors throughout history have done?"

Nonetheless, he played along – perhaps in part because of past friendships, in part because he didn't want to alienate the victors, and in part maybe because he realized that we really were the lesser of two evils. We communicated by secret writing. I took the train from Frankfurt to Hamburg over the next year or so, to meet with him, but the contacts were more social than operationally productive. He wasn't going to stick his neck out very far, or seriously endanger his position for the Americans, and Headquarters finally shut the operation down.

Following my Frankfurt assignment, we were posted to Berlin and I was assigned to Camp Marienfelde. It was the Refugee Reception Center for those fleeing from the East, and dozens defected every day, then stood in line for hours, waiting to be processed.

New boys like me spent some time there debriefing such refugees and picking up whatever stray bits of intelligence they might possess. But the primary reason we were there was to hone our language and area-knowledge skills. By talking to defectors 6 or 7 hours a day, our language skills markedly improved. Sometimes we could even recruit a likely prospect, turn him around and send him back before he was missed, and in exchange we would substantially assist him with his resettlement. The 'benefits of cooperation' were well known to the defectors.

One Saturday the sergeant ushered in a young woman named Ursula. Ushi was her nickname, and she was dead-on gorgeous. Thick, auburn hair, mesmerizing eyes, like Audrey Hepburn, and body to die for.

Ushi was a translator at the Hungarian Military Mission in East Berlin. She had gone in for a routine physical, only to discover that she had a hole between two chambers of her heart. Her doctor recommended surgery, but whispered that if she were planning to defect to the West, she should have her surgery there; the facilities were so much better. She offered to return to East Berlin for a few weeks and work for us, in exchange for our help in expediting her surgery.

I thought that was a great idea – particularly as I would get to be her case officer -- but I did not have the authority to initiate a recruitment.

I went around to see my boss, and in the course of the conversation mentioned this 70 year old crone, who was a translator at the Hungarian mission, and was willing to spy for us in exchange for help with some medical problems. On compassionate grounds, I said, I thought we should take her up on it.

But the boss wasn't buying, and I had to tell Ushi: "Thanks, but no thanks."

What's that old saying: 'Hell hath no fury like a woman scorned?' When I left the compound that evening, Ushi noted the make and license number of my car. For the next few days she scoured the American housing community until she spotted my vehicle, chatted up the housekeepers and nannies, and learned my and Martha's names. For good measure she also noted the license numbers of friends who visited us – mostly fellow case officers, of course. Then, one night, she knocked on our door, handed me the list with a sweet smile, and said: "See? You really should hire me; I'm very good."

We didn't hire her, but we sure got her out of Berlin in a hurry, resettled her in West Germany and arranged for her heart surgery. The point of the story, however, is this: I *knew* that I should have changed license plates before going to the Camp. I *knew* I should have parked five or six blocks away, and checked for surveillance on my way to and from the facility. I knew it in my head, as book-learning; but it hadn't yet penetrated to the gut.

Clearly I was still a novice, and nothing drove that home more forcefully than a case that still haunts me. I had inherited an agent in Gdansk from a case officer who had returned to the States. The agent did not have ready access to the West, and we used couriers and dead-drops to communicate. I recruited one such courier who made several successful trips, but then was caught while illegally crossing the border. The guards set upon him with their dogs, letting them tear chunks of flesh out of him until he died -- of shock, or from loss of blood. Then they dumped his mangled body at the sector boundary on the Friedrichstrasse, at what later became the site of Checkpoint Charlie. The kid was barely 19.

I had failed him. I hadn't trained him well enough in border crossing and escape & evasion techniques. I hadn't made him go over his cover story often enough. I hadn't provided him with a bag full of trinkets that would have allowed him to pass himself off as a smuggler, if caught. That might have gotten him several years in jail — but at least he would still have been alive.

On another occasion, the sergeant ushered an elderly man into my cubicle His hair was disheveled, his eyes unfocused and red from weeping, and despite the unseasonably warm weather, he was shivering. He was pushing an empty baby carriage, and when the sergeant offered to park it in the hall because the cubicle was so small, he clung to it fiercely.

After we had settled him down with a cup of hot tea, laced with rum, he began to tell us his story. It came out in pieces; in disconnected fragments.

He said his name was Mittendorf, and that he was a professor of History at Humboldt University, in the Soviet sector of Berlin. He said that he had married another academic, late in life, and that the two of them had had a single child. As academics, the Mittendorfs had a reasonably comfortable life, but for their child's future they had decided to defect to the West. The Herr Professor, however, was not going to leave East Berlin without his extensive collection of rare books.

Each Sunday he put a layer of books in the baby carriage, put the mattress on top of the books and the baby on top of the mattress. He then wheeled the carriage across the River Spree that separated East from West Berlin, left the books with friends and returned home. This Sunday, however, a border guard had insisted upon inspecting the carriage.

"Anyone who cares more about his books than about his child, deserves neither," the guard said, as he dumped the contents of the carriage – baby and all -- into the river. A young man sunning himself on the river bank stripped off his shirt and prepared to rescue the child, but the guard fired over his head. The screaming baby sank, and the current carried the bundle away.

The guard tore up Mittendorf's identity card and spat, contemptuously: "Go to the West, old man; see if they'll want you."

The professor was frantic. He couldn't go back to the East and he had no way of letting his wife know what had happened. He begged us for help, but there was little we could do other than to get a message through to his wife. CIA wouldn't commit assets to rescuing her; stories like his were all too common.

We liked to think of such incidents as examples of Big, Bad Communism -- but they weren't. Whether it be sexual harassment, the cruelties of the Klan, the brutalization of slaves, or the atrocities of Abu Ghraib -- all are examples of Lord Acton's observation that power corrupts -- and absolute power corrupts absolutely. This was just one more, sorry example.

I was so moved by the tragedy, however that I kept in touch with Dr. Mittendorf, and years later Martha and I looked him up on a vacation trip down Germany's Romantic Road. He was an authority on the Reformation and was teaching at a university. near the restored village of Rothenberg He led us into his favorite sanctuary, the St. Jacob's Church:

"Notice that alter piece," Dr. Mittendorf said, "by Tilman Riemenschneider. It's called the Holy Blood Alter, and he carved it out of a single piece of wood."

"Extraordinary."

"Far more extraordinary than most visitors realize, because Riemenschneider created it *after* he had been jailed by the Inquisition. They broke all of his fingers."

"You mean deliberately?"

"Deliberately, yes. Riemenschneider was a vocal supporter of Martin Luther's, which greatly irritated the Church. They figured that breaking his fingers would be a particularly appropriate punishment for a wood carver and sculptor. But he did his best work *after* his fingers had healed, and in this work he had the last laugh.

"Notice his depiction of the Last Supper. If you view the disciples in the order of their recruitment, they form a lazy 8 – the symbol for infinity -- to celebrate the infinite endurance of Christianity."

"But there are only twelve figures shown – who is missing?"

"Christ is missing. And the central figure is actually Judas, the disciple who sold out Jesus for a handful of silver. The alter piece commemorates the selling out of Christianity by the excesses of the Catholic Church – which is precisely what prompted Martin Luther to break with Rome in the first place."

"I don't recall any reference to this in our guide book."

"Probably because this part of Germany is predominantly Catholic. The city fathers didn't want to destroy Germany's most historic woodcarving – but they didn't want to call attention to its hidden message either."

Dr. Mittendorf had finally been reunited with his wife, but now he seemed to live almost exclusively in the past. Ferreting out such details about the Reformation kept him alive, but when he returned to the present his shoulders sagged and his eyes filled with a great sadness. The Mittendorfs never had another child.

✵✵✵

35

I was far too junior to recognize it at the time, but the tectonic shift in intelligence collection that began after World War II was gathering steam. It was the displacement of human source intelligence (HUMINT) by technology (TECHINT).

Until then, TECHINT had been limited to photo reconnaissance, telephone taps and radio intercepts, but the technical devices were large, limited in capacity and prone to failure. Photo reconnaissance missions were bedeviled by cloud cover, camera failures, and the marginal quality of the films. Sometimes the aircraft themselves were shot down. Radio intercepts were plagued by atmospherics, sun spots and the enemy's use of codes and ciphers. But when it worked, TECHINT had three advantages that human sources could not match: it was fast; it was objective, and it was particularly suitable for the collection of Tactical Intelligence -- the disposition of the enemy's forces and the deployment of his weapons systems.

Technical devices avoid the human problems: they either succeed or they fail, and if the latter, they can be replaced; it's only money. Technical devices are limited by their field of view, but have flawless memories and don't filter what they see through subjective lenses.

In HUMINT, all sides are working with the same raw material – the human source. But in TECHINT, the state of a nation's scientific knowledge, its engineering and its economy make a huge difference. And that's where we had the edge.

The Gdansk source I had inherited produced some useful intelligence, but a month or more elapsed between his observations and the time his reporting reached us. Some agents exaggerated to inflate their importance; some reported what they thought we wanted to hear, rather than what in fact existed. Some were caught, some were shot, some were turned by the Opposition and fed us disinformation, and many just got cold feet and quit.

"Human sources are labor-intensive," our instructor had warned us. "Unless they walk in and volunteer their services, they have to be spotted, vetted, motivated and recruited. They have to be trained in secure communications techniques and provided with believable cover stories – which in turn may have to be backstopped with carefully forged documents. And that's just for starters.

"Because they lead a double life, keeping their fears bottled up, they need an outlet, an oasis: someone upon whom they can vent their frustrations and their fears. As their case officer you become their taskmaster but also their confessor, their counselor -- and their mother. Many will need to see you face to face, at least upon occasion, and you too will want to look them in the eye and assess how they are coping with the strain.

"Your agent's employer may shift him to a new job; he may lose access to the information we need. He may become overconfident and careless about his own security. If he survives the experience (and too many of them don't), he may have to be resettled in a new country, under a new identity, and adjust to customs and to a language that are foreign to him.

"He is almost certain to remain a 'handling problem' for the rest of his life. When he first comes in out of the cold, he will be the center of attention. He will be praised for his bravery and for his resourcefulness. Virtually every wish of his will be granted. But when his intelligence is no longer current, his value will decline. He may be turned over to and managed by a junior or inexperienced case officer. He may become disenchanted with his loss of prestige. He may re-defect."

Those are some of the impediments to agent operations. That said, however, a well-placed human source can be worth his weight in gold. With his access to planning meetings, office scuttlebutt and collegial relationships, he can alert the Intelligence Community to plans and intentions that technical devices cannot divine.

During the Cold War, Soviet science was often on a par with (and in some areas perhaps even superior to) our own. But their engineering and production were plagued by inefficiency, political constraints, excessive centralization, and unbelievable levels of corruption. Here we decidedly had an edge, and therein lay a major competitive advantage that accelerated the shift toward technology.

***

AQUATONE

Edwin Land, founder of the Polaroid Corp., was one of a visionary group of scientists and engineers who served on an advisory panel to CIA. During World War II his company had designed advanced optical systems for the military, and in 1954 he proposed a quantum leap in photo reconnaissance: It would require an aircraft never before built, a camera that did not exist, and a film that had yet to be invented.

Alan Dulles, the Director of Central Intelligence, didn't think those odds sounded very promising, but his friend, Richard M. Bissell, whose family had made its fortune in carpet sweepers, urged him to take the chance. Bissell had amassed an enviable record for his contribution to the execution of the Marshall Plan and was serving as an advisor to the Ford Foundation. Dulles agreed to Edwin Land's proposal, provided that Bissell would transfer to CIA and manage the project.

Bissell set to work with zeal. To avoid Soviet fighters, his relatively slow-moving aircraft would have to to operate at 70,000 feet or better[4], remain aloft for at least six hours and have a range of 2,000 miles or more. All of these specifications were exceeded.

As engine vibration would jiggle the camera and seriously degrade the photography, the plane would have to climb to an altitude of 13 miles, turn off its engine, and function as a glider while the photographs were being taken. Only two airframe companies in the United States had the ability to design such a craft, and Lockheed's 'Skunk Works,' under Kelly Johnson, came up with the better design. Perkin-Elmer, a Rochester-based, advanced optics company was able to create a telephoto lens with the required focal length, and fold it into a box less than two feet square, and Eastman Kodak fabricated an emulsions that could record the necessary detail from these dizzying heights.

Richard Bissell harnessed the capabilities of these three corporations and AQUATONE, one of the Cold War's best kept secrets, was born. Online you can listen to the PBS broadcast in which Thomas Blanton of the National Security Archives talks about the genesis of this project.

The U2 had far reaching consequences in all sorts of unexpected areas, and one is the role which it played in resolving the Yom Kippur War. As we will see, it laid the foundation for the trust and confidence that made the historic Anwar Sadat/Menachem Begin meeting possible.

OPERATION GOLD

As Richard Bissell shepherded AQUATONE through its development in the United States, we were finding it increasingly difficult to conduct agent operations in Berlin.

"Bastards are starting to work together," Bill Harvey grumbled. "I liked it better when they hated each other's guts!"

'Big Bill' Harvey, ex-FBI, was brilliant, imaginative, and tenacious, but 'couth' was not an adjective that readily sprang to mind. He wanted desperately to join the exclusive Blau/Weiss tennis club, to hob-knob with the city's movers & shakers, but that door remained firmly shut. Other, more junior officers, well-spoken and properly brought up, were invited to join, but if they had the brains God gave a mule, they politely declined.

Big Bill had little patience with incompetence, and terrorized junior staff like me. We lived in fear of finding a PSM (Please See Me) with our name on it, tacked to the bulletin board, and if it said SM instead of PSM, we really trembled in our boots. Harvey would stare at the miscreant balefully and say, "OK, motherfucker, where did you screw up?"

Maybe it was a tactic that he brought with him from the FBI, because the miserable worm in front of him would rack his memory for *anything* to confess, however trivial, and Big Bill would look at him pityingly, shake his head in disgust and dismiss him with a wave of the hand.

And then, one day, it happened: "CDL PSM WKH" I knocked timidly on his door and entered. He never looked up from the document he was studying, and I shifted nervously from foot to foot.

"Goddamned Headquarters wants me to tell you they liked your report," he mumbled. "Now get the fuck back to work."

His assessment was correct, however: the KGB and the East German's Ministry for State Security (MfS) were laying their mutual antipathies aside and were cooperating ever more closely with one another. At the same time the Soviets were switching from radio communications (which we were able to intercept) to secure underground telephone and data lines.

During WW-II, the Nazis had laid a network of high-security telephone lines to connect their Military Hqs. (the *Oberkommando der Wehrmacht*, or OKW) with their command centers in the conquered territories. Like a spider's web, these secure lines radiated outward from OKW, in the Karlshorst section of Berlin, to Poland, Czechoslovakia, Hungary, Rumania, Bulgaria, and Austria — even into Moscow itself. As Karlshorst lay in the Soviet sector of Berlin, the Russians simply took over this high-security network and utilized it for their own communications.

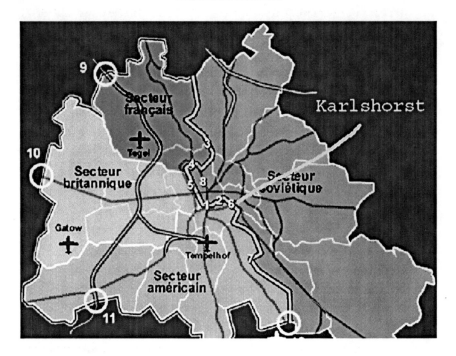

The Karlshorst compound became the headquarters of Soviet Intelligence operations, and all military traffic from their satellite countries flowed <u>first</u> into Berlin, and then out to Moscow through these secure trunk lines. But the Karlshorst compound was only just inside the Soviet boundaries – 1/3rd of a mile from the American sector -- and Harvey came up with a bold plan: to tunnel under the Sector border, locate the trunk lines beneath the Karlshorst compound and monitor <u>all</u> of the Soviet traffic between Moscow and its satellites!

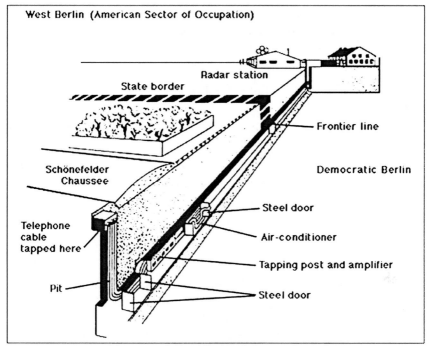

West Berlin (American Sector of Occupation)

Radar station

State border

Frontier line

Schönefelder
Chaussee

Democratic Berlin

Steel door

Telephone
cable
tapped here

Air-conditioner

Tapping post and amplifier

Pit

Steel door

Diagram of the Altglienicke spy tunnel

The Joint Chiefs authorized the US Army's Corps of Engineers to construct a radar installation on our side of the border – but it was also a cover for the proposed tunnel. 24 feet below the surface, it was the length of six football fields. A railroad track ran its entire length, to facilitate the removal of 130,000 cu. ft. of dirt, enough to fill 48 standard boxcars. It was air-conditioned because the heat from the 256 pre-amplifiers that would route the telephone taps to the banks of recorders in the American Sector would melt any snow that might fall on the streets above. (The transistor had not yet been invented; all electronic deices were vacuum-tube operated). Among other things, the tunnel was equipped with washing machines and showers so that the mud-soaked workers could clean up before emerging.

It was a joint operation with MI-6, and once the tunnel had been completed, the British dug a vertical shaft, intercepted the trunk lines, and made the 256 taps. Work began in February of 1954 and the tunnel went operational 14 months later.

440,000 telephone and teletype messages were intercepted; 10,500 intelligence reports were produced from these intercepts and over 1,200 of those were of Top Secret caliber.

But the Soviets were aware of Operation Gold from the day it was planned.

George Blake, MI-6's Hamburg station chief at the time I was being trained for assignment there, had volunteered to work for the KGB many years before, and by 1954 had become the deputy chief of MI-6's Berlin Station. A brilliant and talented officer, he was so good and so highly regarded by both the British and the Americans that he was generally expected to become the future head of MI-6.

The Soviets knew it, and realized that if they rolled up the operation, they would risk compromising this most valuable source. At the same time, with thousands of messages flowing across these tapped lines every day, any attempt to use them for deception purposes would become apparent very quickly.

Nikita Khrushchev himself ordered the KGB to let the operation proceed, but ultimately found the intelligence loss to be too costly. The tunnel was 'discovered', and not long thereafter Blake was compromised, convicted and sentenced to 42 years in Britain's Wormwood Scrubs prison. Five years later, however, an IRA revolutionary arranged to plant a getaway car in a convenient spot. Blake scaled an 18' wall, dropped to the ground, badly spraining an ankle, but hobbled to the car and made his escape. He then contacted his old case officer and was spirited out of the UK to the USSR.

This 1991 photo shows Blake (in white) addressing a group of retired KGB officers in Moscow. His case officer, Gen. Sergei Kondrashev, is on his right. In 1997, Kondrashev and Dave Murphy, former Chief of Base, Berlin, co-authored *Battleground Berlin*[5] which covers this case in great detail. And Maj. Gen. Oleg Kalugin, who was in charge of all of the KGB's operations against the Americans, is now co-chairman of the International Spy Museum in Washington. How the world has changed!

We had some unofficial contact with our British and French counterparts, too, and each year staged a mini-America's Cup regatta that pitted the Allied forces against each other on Berlin's Wansee. Our coach, Herr August Thieme, was a German Olympic sailor who spoke passable English, but lapsed into his native tongue when upset with our performance. And I was often the cause of his distress. I was an avid sailor, but a lousy tactician, and usually ended up among the losers. This year however was the exception.   .

It was hot and sultry; the winds had been light all day and died completely as we neared the finish line. By some fluke I was in the lead; a Brit was some fifty yards behind, but was slowly gaining on me because my crew, a Mrs. Anne Parks, had nodded off; she was supposed to be tending the jib.

It was too much for our coach on shore; Herr Thieme saw what was happening and was stomping up and down in frustration. Suddenly he picked up his megaphone and bellowed across the water: "Fock, Mrs. Parks. Fock, Mrs. Parks!"

Fock is the German word for jib, and what the coach was trying to impart to the dear lady was that she needed to wake up and get with it, else we would lose the race. But Anne's German left much to be desired, and as she stood up in the boat to express her outrage, the lightest zephyr caught the sail and swung it lazily across the boat. The boom bonked her on the head; she lost her balance, went over board, and in that moment confronted me with a major, ethical dilemma: For if I stopped to pick her up, the Brit would overhaul me and win the race. But if I didn't, the wretched woman might drown.

Without a moment's hesitation, I put America's honor ahead of human life, sailed on and won the race, while the Brit courteously stopped and helped the lady out of the water. The race committee promptly disqualified me for finishing without a crew and the whole club shunned me for my boorish and heartless behavior. The British were declared the winners and were honored for their conduct -- while all the while their Deputy Chief of Mission, George Blake, was a KGB agent, compromising our most valuable operation!

✵✵✵

By the end of our first tour, I was thoroughly hooked, and had no interest at all in returning to 'civilian' life. Martha, too, was captivated and participated in a number of operational support tasks. In surveillance cases, for example, a man alone is viewed as more of a threat than one accompanied by a female; a woman can follow a female suspect into a restroom, and when a wife is involved in operational tasks, she is more likely to understand and be tolerant of her husband's erratic absences. It was for those reasons that many Station Chiefs encouraged their officers to involve their spouses.

A surveillance detection tactic popular among some of the satellite agents was to head straight for the lingerie section of a department store and to tarry there, ostensibly picking out a sexy little confection for a girl-friend. A male surveillant hanging about in the same department would stand out like a sore thumb, but a female could easily blend. Martha did so on several occasions.

JESTER:

This case was typical of the bread & butter operations we dealt with. A young woman we'll call Trudi was a secretary in the East German's Ministry for Heavy Machinery. Because she had no access to classified materials, she was able to travel between East and West Berlin, and she did so regularly to visit her girl friend, Brigitte. But in mid 1959 Trudi told her friend that she would not be returning; she had been notified that she was being reassigned to the *STASI*[6] – the Ministry for State Security – and its clerical employees were not permitted to visit West Berlin.

Six months later, however, Trudi popped up again – this time in tears. "The man is a pig," she complained to her friend, Brigitte, speaking about her new boss. "He paws every woman under 35 and mauls me every time he can get me alone in the files room."

"Just quit, Trudi; you're so efficient you'd have no trouble getting another job. Or defect; there's plenty of work here."

"But not in West Berlin..."

"Well, no; maybe not in Berlin: we already have more defectors here than we can handle. But you'd be resettled in Hanover or Frankfurt or other parts of Germany, and they are crying for good people."

"Gitte – I can't leave Berlin. My whole family is here, and they aren't going to come over; you know that. Papi and Mami are almost 80 and are drawing a pension; Horst is about to get married.

"The pig I work for is a big cheese in the *STASI*, you know. Speaks fluent Russian and is the liaison officer to the KGB or some such security outfit. If he blackballed me, my whole family would be skunked.

"Besides, the job's got a lot of perks, and what the hell, Gitte, I'm not exactly a virgin."

"Coming to West Berlin is one of those perks?"

"Yeah. He sends me here with a shopping list, and because of it I have a special pass. He claims that he is buying this stuff to outfit agents the *STASI* is sending to West, but half of the goods he has me buy he resells at exorbitant prices on the Black Market.

"The good news," she added, "is that I can get to see you from time to time. And load up on Tampax, of course."

It was well known that tampons manufactured in the East were markedly inferior to those available in the West, and women with access to West Berlin bought them in large quantities for themselves, and for their friends. Trudi was no exception.

On her next visit, Brigitte took Trudi to the Café Kranzler, on the Kurfürstendamm, Berlin's Rodeo Drive. And there they 'just happened' to run into one of Brigitte's girl friends, who was having coffee with a Swiss engineer studying at the Technische Hochschule — Berlin's Polytechnic Institute. Only he wasn't Swiss and he wasn't an engineer; it was I.

We laughed and chatted for over an hour and agreed to meet again. In time — thanks largely to her boss' boorish behavior and insufferable arrogance -- I was able to recruit Trudi as an access agent, train her in surveillance avoidance techniques and in communication alternatives. JESTER was the name assigned to her boss, the ultimate target of the operation.

A typical German bureaucrat, JESTER took meticulous notes of his meetings with his KGB counterpart, and Trudi typed them up. She made an extra carbon copy of such notes, and smuggled them out of the office in her underwear. She photographed them at home with a small camera, and then destroyed the incriminating carbons. Occasionally she also managed to photograph some of the phony vouchers her boss signed to embezzle funds from his service.

The special camera's tiny cassette was smaller than a single peanut in its shell, and stored 50 exposures. On the day of our scheduled contact, Trudi took a fresh tampon from its wrappings, cut out its middle third, and replaced it with the cassette. She stuffed the assembly back into its applicator, the applicator back into its paper sleeve and added it to the other tampons in her purse.

Brigitte visited the rest room in Berlin Zoo's S-Bahn station, removed the spindle from a roll of toilet paper and replaced it with one that had been specially modified as a concealment device.

Later that day Trudi took the S-Bahn to West Berlin, went to the same restroom and hid just the cassette inside the spindle. She flushed the modified tampon and its applicator down the toilet, and made a small chalk mark on a lamppost a few blocks away: a vertical mark signaled that the drop had been made; a diagonal mark indicated that she wanted to have a meeting with me – an emergency measure. She spent the next hour or two shopping for the items on her boss' list.

When Brigitte spotted Trudi's signal, she retrieved the drop and re-placed the original spindle. She made her own mark on a second lamppost, and unless the mark was a diagonal one, signaling that I needed to meet with Trudi, she would return to East Berlin with her purchases.

For several months we were able to monitor the preparations for the infamous Berlin Wall. Her product, along with collateral reporting from other sources, gave the National Security Council time to consider what America's response would be, once the East German's made their move. Christian Herter was the Secretary of State at the time, later replaced by the hawkish Dean Rusk, when Kennedy assumed the presidency, and the initial sentiment was to take a strong, confrontational stand against the so-called German Democratic Republic, and its Soviet masters.

But the more he thought about it the more Dean Rusk concluded that the Wall would in fact become a strong propaganda weapon for the West. Educated and ambitious Eastern Europeans were fleeing in droves. Bottle them up behind a wall, Rusk argued, and growing dissatisfaction would ultimately cause the kettle to explode. It would also be a PR disaster for the East, he predicted, proving to the world that the only way to keep good people in the "workers' paradise" was to seal them up in a cage.

In the long run Rusk's assessment proved to be right, but in the short run the Wall looked like a diplomatic defeat for the United States: If America were unwilling to stand up for her rights in Berlin, the world wondered, where could she be trusted to hold the line?

President Kennedy recalled Gen. Lucius D. Clay from retirement, and at 0645 on Sunday, August 20th, 1961he led an armored column in full battle dress 110 miles through occupied East Germany and into West Berlin; there they were greeted by Vice President Lyndon Johnson. East German police, border guards and Soviet troops looked on in amazement, but did not try to stop the advance, and West Berliners were overjoyed by America's resolve. For the next three and a half years this march was repeated every three months, as US commanders rotated troops into and out of Berlin.

I imagine we would have continued using Trudi indefinitely, but the *STASI* tightened its security practices, and clerical employees were subject to random body searches when they left the office. Her parents were no longer living, and she had few ties to bind her to the GDR. I was back in Washington by then, but she signaled that she wanted out, and the Agency resettled her in the West.

***

Like her mother, Martha was bi-polar; her condition remained unrecognized and didn't manifest itself until late in 1960; by then I had a full complement of agents and often worked 14 hours a day.

In Berlin the tanks were rumbling as the military maneuvered for a confrontation that many regarded as inevitable. -- the opening salvos of the events that would lead to the creation of the Berlin Wall. Martha became increasingly tense; she couldn't sleep; she was certain that the Russians were spying on her every move, and were plotting to kidnap our children. She broke down and had to be evacuated to Frankfurt for hospitalization, then back to the United States once she had been stabilized.

I turned my cases over to fellow officers and accompanied her to Washington, and I cannot speak highly enough of the way the Agency's resources were mobilized to help her. We were provided with temporary housing, with day care for the children, and were referred to an excellent psychiatrist — much of this at the Agency's expense.

***

As my career as a Clandestine Services case officer sputtered to a halt, Martha's condition worsened; for the next five years she would zoom from the depths of depression to periods of manic frenzy. It was a ghastly period and it tore the family apart. In her manic phases she would go berserk and would have to be hospitalized. In her depressed state she would lie on the couch in a fetal position, disconnected from her family and from everything around her.

Today we know that these bi-polar conditions are caused by a chemical imbalance, but we didn't know it then. I yelled at her, shook her, screamed at her to 'just snap out of it,' and the children witnessed it all. It couldn't go on that way; we were tearing ourselves to shreds. Martha's parents came and took the children to their home in Long Island for a year. They were spared the worst of it, but even at that I was amazed at their resilience.

Martha was hospitalized repeatedly. Psychiatry didn't help. Electroshock therapy didn't help. Thorazine turned her into a virtual zombie and didn't really help

I don't think our marriage could have survived, had it not been for Beulah. She was a mountain of a black woman — 350 lbs. at least — and a wonderful, unflappable oasis of calm. She was raising two grandchildren that her daughter had run off and abandoned, and she was her family's sole source of income. She had cared for Martha's mother in her manic-depressive phases, and knew just how to calm us down when our world was coming apart at the seams. She loved us unconditionally, as we loved her.

Beulah had two long scars on her arms, and when I asked her one day how she had acquired them, she said that she had taken some razors away from a couple of boys who were fighting. "How old were the boys, Beulah?"

"Oh, twenty-four, twenty-five."

But diabetes was already taking control of her life; One of her legs was amputated. Then the other. Ultimately she lost her eyesight, and some months later she died.

A few psychiatrists across the nation were authorized by the National Institute of Mental Health to experiment with a new substance called lithium carbonate. Martha's doctor was one of them. It was a miracle drug for us, and in a matter of weeks her condition stabilized.

We got our lives back.

***

II

The Technical Connection

Luck had stepped in when I returned from Berlin, and I was summoned by a Dr. Sidney Gottlieb, the head of what was then called the Technical Services Division (TSD). His group was responsible for creating the technical devices used for espionage, deploying them in denied areas and training agents to use them.

While TSD's 400+ engineers and technicians were extraordinarily clever and competent, few of them had had any first-hand experience as case officers, recruiting and handling agents. As I was fresh from the field, Dr. Gottlieb asked me to develop training courses that would more closely marry technology and Operations.

Photography, lock picking, the emplacement of audio devices, the surreptitious opening of envelopes — all of these skills were being taught in classrooms and in controlled environments; the students learned and could demonstrate their skills, but really didn't have to worry about being caught. Case officers, too, who would be calling upon our guys for such technical support when they reached the field, were sent overseas without ever having experienced the tension of a surreptitious entry operation. All that struck me as being somewhat sterile; the acid test was missing.

As our children were up in Long Island with their grandparents, and Martha was in a mental ward, I decided to turn our house into a training base. We lived on a quiet, residential street in Northwest Washington, cheek by jowl with our neighbors. Pulling off a surreptitious entry and carrying out a series of operational tasks, right under the noses of those neighbors, would make for a fitting, final exam.

The students had two weeks to plan and execute the entry. They had to case the area, establish the neighbors' activity patterns, and determine how and where they would break into our house. They had to develop their communications plans, prepare their escape routes and decide where they would deploy protective surveillance to cover them during the entry.

A couple of days before the scheduled entry, I locked up the house, told my neighbors that I'd be gone for a few days, and moved to a motel to stay out of their way.

On the night of the entry, one of the team members picked the locks, and a second disabled the alarm system. The rest of the team then entered and went to work. They had to open a variety of envelopes, photograph their contents, and reseal them. They had to conceal an audio transmitter in the telephone, conceal additional audio devices in the living and dining rooms, and insure that their signals could be heard at the listening post. They had to do all this without showing any lights, clean up every trace of their visit, reset the alarm, re-lock the doors and exit. If they were caught they might spend an uncomfortable hour or two at the local police station, but better that they make their mistakes here than in the field.

Most of the exercises went off without a hitch, for these guys and gals were good. But one incident was notable:

The team had done its job and was just about to exit, when a car pulled up in front of our house. It was our neighbor's daughter, being brought home by her boyfriend. She suggested parking there for a little smooching, because she knew that we were away.

Trapped inside the target, the team chafed and fretted while the car's shock absorbers got a real workout. Dawn was less than an hour away, and the team was worried it might have to spend the whole day in the house before it could make a safe exit.

Their commander was in the listening post, about six blocks away, directing the team's activities and listening to their growing distress. He finally called the police with an anonymous complaint about *"..unseemly goings-on — right in front of God and everyone -- and on a public street, too!"* but neglected to inform the team that he was doing so. The police obligingly sent a patrol car to break up the engagement, but when the team saw a cruiser pull up in front of the house, its red and blue lights flashing, they almost freaked out.

"Man," said one team member during the post mortem, "I thought my pants would never dry."

✳✳✳

Overseeing a group of 400 or more creative engineers and technicians is a bit like herding cats, and Sid Gottlieb decided he needed an Executive Officer to help. He tapped me for the job.

An EXO is a staff officer; he commands no troops, but serves the boss to insure that the trains are on track and on time. It was a delicate balance, for I could not usurp or undercut line authorities, but had to insure that Dr. Gottlieb was fully briefed on the operations being supported, and was made aware of all potential problem areas.

Most clandestine operations drew upon TSD's personnel devices to one extent or another; and the feedback from those operations showed us how well we were doing, and where we needed to improve. At the same time, the nation was booming along, developing more and more technologies that our engineers could exploit and apply to clandestine operations. As EXO, I was sitting at the confluence of those two streams.

Some examples of operations TSD supported, both before and during my tenure as EXO.

COBRA:

The technician watched the agent trying to photograph a document. "One of them Liberal Arts types", he thought to himself disparagingly, "who can't even manage a can opener."

The agent was using a Minox camera, and making a proper mess of it: His elbow would get into the picture, or his thumb would cover a part of the lens, or he'd have the document partly in light and partly in shadow. Invariably his focus was off by a country mile. In the early 1960's, the Minox was a classic spy camera, a trifle larger than a Dunhill cigarette lighter; its film was very small, and it didn't tolerate a lot of error. It was the same device that Trudi was using in the JESTER case

Our technical officer had been hauled out of bed at 3:00 AM and taken to a safehouse. He had been summoned for the express purpose of analyzing the agent's procedures and correcting his technique.

The correction part was simple: the tech had the agent place his elbows on the table, in a comfortable position, and told him to rest his chin on his folded hands. That would allow him to hold the camera between his palms, and cup them around the instrument should someone unexpectedly enter the room. The tech then carefully measured the distance to the tabletop, set the focus precisely to that distance and cemented the focusing dial so that it could not be changed. He computed the exposure for the illumination that would be provided by a 60 Watt bulb, and cemented the exposure control as well. You pulled the camera apart to cock it, pressed the shutter release to take the picture, and pushed the camera back together again to advance the film. Pull, Click, Push; Pull, Click, Push -- even a Liberal Arts type should be able to manage that.

Only much later did we learn the agent's identity: he was a Colonel in the Soviet Army's Intelligence Branch – the GRU - and one of the great unsung heroes of the Cold War. There have been several books about him, and some of his diary has been published, but the world is generally unaware of the immense debt it owes this man. He has been aptly called "The Spy Who Saved the World."

Oleg Penkovsky was born in 1919, the son of a Czarist officer who fought against the Bolsheviks in the 1917 Civil War. He graduated at the top of his class from the Frunze Military Academy, received additional training at the Diplomatic-Military Institute and became an expert in rocket and missile technology at the Dzerzinsky Academy.

He was assigned to the GRU, but while he was brilliant, he advanced very slowly. Far less able contemporaries rose rapidly in rank, while Penkovsky was passed over again and again. His father had fought the Communists in 1917; his mother was an intellectual, and the Soviet leadership deeply distrusted such backgrounds:

In August of 1960, fed up with the Soviet system, he made his approach: Two American students were waiting in line at the In-Tourist office in Moscow to obtain tickets to the Bolshoi. Penkovsky observed their purchase, and followed them to their hotel. Flashing his credentials, he obtained the names of these students from their hotel clerk, as well as the other particulars recorded in their passports, returned to his office and checked their names against GRU and KGB files.

That evening, as the students headed for the theatre, he followed them again. Their path took them through Gorky Park and across a footbridge that was poorly lighted; in one lamppost in particular the bulb had burned out, creating a pool of darkness. When they returned from the Bolshoi and crossed that bridge again, he brushed by them as they traversed the pool of darkness and slipped an envelope into their hands. "Please," he said, "for the American Ambassador" and melted into the darkness.

Penkovsky was so bright, so able, and so likable, that among the professionals – as opposed to the political hacks – he was highly regarded. Gen. Serov, head of the GRU, unburdened himself to Penkovsky over many a shared liter of Vodka, as did General Vorensov, in charge of all Soviet missile development and a member of the Supreme Military Council that was chaired by Khrushchev.

Both of these able and experienced officers distrusted Chairman Khrushchev, his mercurial nature, his tendency to shoot from the hip, and think afterwards, and both trusted Penkovsky enough to make their feelings known to him.

Penkovsky became increasingly worried about the future of the *Rodina* – the motherland. From his pals, Generals Serov and Vorensov, as well as his own position he had a pretty accurate appreciation of the Soviet and American missile capabilities, and knew that the USSR's were wanting.

From Gen. Vorensov he learned that Khrushchev had little respect for President Kennedy because of the Bay of Pigs fiasco. The ill-conceived plan to topple Fidel Castro that Kennedy had inherited from the Eisenhower administration might have succeeded if the president had not withheld air support at the last moment. Khrushchev was a gambler and a bluffer; he would have gone for it.

For Penkovsky, the stakes were too high for gambling. The Soviet Union had barely survived the loss of 20 million of its citizens in the Great Patriotic War, and Penkovsky was convinced that a nuclear exchange with the United States would wipe out the USSR completely, if not the entire world. That was why he gave his letter to the two American students.

The Americans, however, weren't buying. James Jesus Angleton, at that time the head of CIA's Counter Intelligence Staff, had been a personal friend of Kim Philby during the War, a close associate of Burgess and MacLean, and initially had been taken in by George Blake as well. All of them were in fact Soviet agents. Angleton was convinced that Penkovsky was a provocation, and disapproved operational contact. Penkovsky's letter was ignored.

Penkovsky made a second approach, this time through a British businessman named Grevil Wynn. He passed the message on to Britain's Secret Service, MI-6, which bypassed Angleton and brought it straight to Richard Helms, the Director of Central Intelligence. He approved the contact.

The first operational meeting with Penkovsky took place on 21 April 1961, in Paris. Present were Joe Bulik, the lead CIA case officer, George Kiesevalter, an extraordinary officer who spoke fluent Russian, and John Shergold, the British case officer. That meeting lasted three hours – they discussed his access, his motivation, how often he was able to travel to the West and how they would communicate with him.

He had brought along some photographs he had taken of documents to which he had access, and apologized for not being much of a photographer. That's how TSD, got involved. We fixed up a Minox camera for him and welded everything into position.

As mentioned, the camera's tiny cassette holds 50 exposures, and over the next 18 months he exposed over 200 cassettes, producing some 10,000 frames of mostly excellent photography.

Occasionally on Sundays he would go for a stroll in Gorky Park. Mrs. Frank Chisholm, wife of the British MI-6 officer, took her baby to the park as well, and Russians, who love babies (and blond babies in particular), would stop and admire the child. They would chuck it under the chin, make silly goo-goo noises, and Penkovsky was only one of many who did so. In the process he slipped his exposed cassettes under the baby's mattress.

His production was prodigious – too prodigious. He photographed missile manuals, test results, telemetry reports, drawings of their launch pads and specifications of their associated radars. He exploded the myth of Soviet missile superiority, and saved the American taxpayer billions of dollars of Defense expenditures. Many of the missiles the Russians displayed in their Red Square parades were simply prototypes; some in fact were papier-mâché mock-ups, and among the few that were operational, the failure rate of their test launches was horrendous; it wasn't because their science was bad but because their production facilities were so sloppy, and laced with corruption.

His case officer told him to cool it: he was taking too many risks; the KGB would get on to him. But the GRU held the KGB in great disdain. "Gum shoes" Penkovsky called them. Thick-headed thugs who hadn't been able to meet the GRU's high standards.

And then one day Gen. Vorensov told him that Khrushchev had decided to emplace the SA-4 and SA-5 missiles in Cuba. In due course, Penkovsky's photography included shipping manifests, bills of lading, names of vessels and details of how the missiles would be carried and concealed. He didn't know where, specifically, they would be sited, but armed with that detailed information, the U-2s began to scour the islands, and the photo interpreters knew exactly what to look for. The tense *Thirteen Days of October*, during which the president confronted the Soviet Union and the world teetered on the brink of nuclear war, were the result.

It should have been a great personal triumph for Penkovsky, but he was no longer around to bask in his success. The gum shoes he had dismissed with such disdain had acquired the apartment directly above his. Reportedly they lowered a video camera from their window, to look into the window below, and caught him in the act of photographing documents. He was arrested, tortured, tried and sentenced to death. Some say he was dispatched with a bullet to the back of his head. Others say that Khrushchev was so furious that he ordered Penkovsky be fed, alive, into a crematorium, before an assembly of GRU and KGB officers. It would serve as an object lesson to other potential traitors.

Joe Bulik, Penkovsky's American case officer, is convinced we could have saved him[7]. Anticipating that the agent might eventually be caught, he had prepared packets of seriously incriminating materials on four, very high-ranking Soviet officials, and wanted to threaten to make these public unless Penkovsky were released. But the White House would not agree, and Bulik says he never forgave the president for not making the attempt. The pivotal player of the Cold War, Penkovsky truly was the "Spy Who Saved the World," We owed him at least that.

Maj. Gen. Oleg Kalugin, Chief of the KGB's Counter Espionage Operations, disagrees. "It would not have made a difference." Khrushchev was too angry. He realized that the intense embarrassment of the Cuban Missile Crisis would spell his downfall – as indeed it did. But our failure to even <u>attempt</u> the rescue of so valuable a source sent a chilling message to other potential walk-ins.

This was slam-dunk Intelligence; Intelligence as good as it will ever get. Soviet intentions as expressed by Gens. Serov and Vorensov, and reported to us by a well-placed agent. Manuals and manifests, photographed by Penkovsky, showing what was being shipped to Cuba, and U2 photography that corroborated the agent's reports, proving beyond the shadow of a doubt that the missile sites were being built.

It was a perfect blend of human source and technical intelligence; we had the Soviets dead to rights, and the United States prepared to carry out a pre-emptive strike against Cuba. 180,000 troops were mobilized in preparation for such a strike, to be preceded by 1,080 air sorties.

Just then a conciliatory message from Khrushchev came in over the Hot Line. It said that if the United States would promise not to invade Cuba, the Soviets would dismantle and remove their missiles. But within a couple of hours a second, hard-line message came in over the same channel, threatening massive retaliation against the United States if Cuba were attacked. Which of the two messages was to be believed?

Gen. Curtis E. LeMay, the Air Force's Chief of Staff and other major voices in the US, called for a pre-emptive strike, but just one man around the president's table [former Ambassador to Moscow] Llewellyn "Tommy" Thompson argued that the conciliatory letter was the one that reflected Khrushchev real intent.

During his years as America's ambassador to the Soviet Union, he had come to know the Soviet leader well. 'Khrushchev is looking for a face-saving way to back down, he argued. 'If he can tell his people that he has saved Cuba from being invaded by the US, and get the United States to dismantle missile bases in Turkey that are threatening the USSR, he will be satisfied.' To Curtis LeMay's disgust, Kennedy accepted Tommy Thompson's judgment and chose instead to blockade Cuba. Khrushchev abided by his promise, and the crisis ended.

Thirty years later we learned that President Kennedy had made the right call. Thirty years later Secretary McNamara sat down with Fidel Castro and found that our 'perfect Intelligence' was just a little bit off: the Russians were indeed constructing missile sites, as Penkovsky had reported, but 90 of the missiles were already operational and armed with nuclear warheads. They had the range to reach as far as Denver, Colorado, and in the event of a pre-emptive strike, the Soviet commander had Khrushchev's authority to launch them. As a shaken Secretary McNamara remarked when reflecting upon his meeting with Castro: "We came that close." You can listen to his exact words on his excellent video, *The Fog of War.*

✳✳✳

THE ROAD TO HELL...

"....is paved with good intentions," we have been told, and sometimes the best ideas have unintended consequences. The 'testimony' quoted below is fictitious, but it captures both the substance and the spirit of what actually occurred:

Testimony before the Select Committee on Government Operations, February 14th, 1975

"Let me make sure I have properly understood your testimony, sir."

"Yes, Senator."

"First you approached the postmaster of the (REDACTED) mail facility and asked him to divert certain mailbags."

"That is correct, Senator"

"You moved these bags to a secure location, and you opened them."

"That was my testimony, yes sir."

"Although you knew that it was against the law."

"Technically, yes."

"And then you proceeded to open all of the letters in these bags."

"Not all of them, Senator, but many of them."

"And one of those letters happened to be addressed to me."

"Yes, Senator Church, by chance it was."

"By chance?"

"It was not our intent to intercept your mail, Senator."

"But in fact you did."

"That is correct, Senator."

"And having opened the envelopes, you photographed and read the letters, resealed the envelopes and returned them to the mail channel."

"That is only partially correct, Senator. We neither read nor photographed the letters."

"You didn't? Then what in God's name were you up to?"

"I can't answer that question in open session, Senator. But the Senate's Sub-Committee on Intelligence was fully briefed."

"And they authorized you to open my letters?"

"No sir. As I testified, that was inadvertent."

"You had a warrant for this activity?"

"Er, no sir. The Attorney General advised us that we did not require a warrant, as the activity was not directed against a specific person"

***

Before the downing of Gary Powers ended the U2 flights over the Soviet Union, and before satellite coverage began, CIA had become aware of a highly secret facility, in the steppes of Kazakhstan, at Semipalatinsk. The analysts' attention had been drawn to it by the five concentric rings of barbed wire surrounding the facility – a horizontal security measure that the Soviets reserved for their most sensitive sites. A series of agents had been dispatched in an attempt to learn what was going on, but with little success, and a secretary was busy typing up the most recent status report.

An original and three copies were required, and she fished a piece of bond paper, three flimsies and three sheets of carbon paper out of her drawer. Fifteen minutes later the report was done – an original, but with only *two* copies. She had put one of the carbon sheets in backwards, and the third 'copy' was actually on the back of the original.

When her boss picked up the report the following morning, the carbon residue on the back of the page smudged his fingers. He frowned as he cleaned them with his handkerchief, and then stopped:

"Get Hendrix in here," he ordered. "On the double!"

***

It took the better part of a year to set up the VANESSA[8] project, and to clear it with our sister agencies. The Justice Department had to be brought on board. The National Meteorological Service. The Postmaster

General, the National Security Advisor, the Vice President and the CEO of a major US company.

Continuing Testimony before the Senate's Select Committee on Government Operations

"We are in executive session today, sir, and you are still under oath."

"Thank you, Senator."

"You may proceed."

"Senators, needless to say this was a very tightly held project. It is true that we intercepted over 10,000 letters, sent to the United States from the Soviet Union, and...."

"Addressed to US citizens?"

"Addressed to US <u>residents</u>, sir. I don't know how many of them may have been US citizens."

"Go on."

"It is also true, as I testified yesterday, that we had no interest in the written messages they contained."

"No interest?"

"None whatever, Senator. We were interested only in the residue on the backs of those letters."

"Would you clarify that, please?"

"When you place a piece of paper on your table, Senator, and write on it, it will pick up particles of any dirt or dust that may be on the table's surface. And unless you wipe down that surface very carefully before you start, there <u>will</u> be particulate matter that will be picked up. Just as though there had been a piece of carbon paper, upside down, on the table top."

"And your interest was in the particulate matter?"

"Yes sir. Because the Soviets paid zero attention to pollution control, particulate matter in the smoke that belched from their stacks was carried downwind and settled on surfaces indoors and out. We opened the letters, pressed them against transfer sheets and then returned the letters to the mail. We ran our tests on the transfer sheets."

"You opened all the letters from the Soviet Union?"

"No sir – only from urban areas, downwind of selected factories. The Met Office was able to help pinpoint the most promising urban areas, based on global wind patterns, and the Post Office was able to single out the mailbags from those centers."

"Why did you have to open the envelopes at all? Why not just test the envelopes themselves?"

"Because those envelopes rubbed up against one another in the mailbags. Our samples would have been both diluted and contaminated. We also would not have known where the residue had come from. The letters *inside* the envelopes, however, remained pristine and were site-specific.

"And this project was successful?"

"At the time, sir, it was all we had."

"And you are doing this still?"

"Senator, that goes beyond what I am authorized to discuss."

Six months later the Church Committee proposed, and the Congress passed, a comprehensive set of regulations regarding the intercept of foreign communications. Its expanded version, signed into law by President Carter in 1978, became known the FISA Act.

***

RUSSIAN INTENTIONS:

The Cold War may be over, but it would be a mistake to underestimate the Russians, or their aspirations. They are a smart people. They led the post-war world in rocketry: they were the first in space and were able to lift far heavier payloads into orbit than were we. They led the world in metallurgy and developed titanium alloys that allowed their submarines to travel at underwater speeds in excess of 60 knots — which in those days I believe was significantly faster than our own. They armor-plated their tanks with alloys that our anti-tank missiles (at the time) could not penetrate. While they never matched us in micro-miniaturization, their bugging of the great American seal over our ambassador's desk in Moscow, in 1946, displayed an innovative application of technology that was well ahead of our own. We didn't discover the bug until six years later.

For years thereafter they flooded the US Embassy in Moscow with a radio frequency emanation — the so-called Moscow Signal -- and as of the time I retired we had not yet been able to determine its purpose. The

Russians take education far more seriously than do we, and they are very ambitious. They would like a turn at being Top Dog, and in 2005 the *Manchester Guardian* reported that Russian espionage in the UK was back to Cold War levels. I earnestly hope that we are continuing our collection efforts in the former Soviet states, but I suspect that it is, at best, at a much reduced level.

***

No leader felt the USSR's second-rate status more strongly than did Leonid Brezhnev. He believed that the USSR had been humiliated during the Cuban missile crisis of 1962. Had Khrushchev stuck to his guns, Brezhnev believed, the United States could have been forced out of Berlin and possibly out of Western Europe. Incredibly poor stewards of their own economy, the Soviets badly needed to control the productive capacity of Western Europe to counteract the power of the United States. Under Brezhnev, at least two more attempts would be made to emasculate what the Soviets called 'The Main Enemy;" both would bring us dangerously close to a nuclear confrontation:

HONOR

The year was 1967 and with Leonid Brezhnev's encouragement, the Egyptians and the Syrians launched the Yom Kippur war, crossing into and soundly thrashing the Israelis. Seeing their critically important ally threatened with destruction, the United States launched the most massive airlift in its history to supply the Israeli forces with weapons.

Meanwhile, half way around the world, a TSD technician was fitting an agent with a disguise. The agent was a top official in a country that had close ties to the Egyptians, and he had received a disturbing report from his Military's Chief of Staff: Soviet advisors to the Egyptian forces were constructing facilities to store nuclear-tipped artillery shells. These tactical nuclear weapons were being supplied because America's intervention was tilting the balance of the Yom Kippur war toward the Israelis.

The agent's report was immediately dispatched to Washington by cable[9]. At the same time, CIA's gamma ray detectors in the Dardanelle Straits noted that Soviet ships were leaving the Black Sea, carrying nuclear materials, and were transiting the Bosporus on their way to the Mediterranean. Putting the two reports together, Henry Kissinger and the National Security Council placed the military on high alert, and in a Hot-Line call to Secretary Brezhnev, President Nixon made it clear that any use of nuclear weaponry would trigger a response in kind.

The element of surprise was gone, and Brezhnev's plan suffered another setback. Both leaders agreed to scale back their support to their respective allies, and now a face-saving way had to be found to extricate themselves from this involvement.

As mentioned earlier, the United States allowed its U2 photography to serve as an honest broker to assure the Egyptians and the Israelis that both were abiding by their promises to withdraw.

The capabilities of the U2's camera were a closely guarded secret, and never before to my knowledge had unexpurgated U2 photography been released to a foreign power. But Dino Brugioni, who headed the photo-interpreter team, argued strongly in favor of doing so. Said Dino: "Man, if we can get peace in the Middle East by sacrificing one damn camera, let's do it."[10]

Cuba was the first, and this was the second time that the Soviets' ambitions to overwhelm the West had been thwarted. Brezhnev was not one to forgive or forget such setbacks, and shortly thereafter he laid plans for an even more ambitious stroke:

***

GULL

At 4:30 PM on August 11th,1972 the sailing vessel *Legya* nosed gently into her berth in Wilhelmshafen, West Germany. Her white hull gleamed in the late afternoon sun, and her brightwork shone. Her home port was Gdansk, and along with the yellow Quarantine Flag international maritime law requires upon entry, she flew the courtesy flag of the Federal Republic of Germany from her starboard spreader.

Clutching the ship's papers, her skipper stepped ashore to attend to the formalities of entry, and thereafter the crew was given shore leave.

There were eight of them. They were dressed as tourists, but they were in fact spies. All were officers of the Polish General Staff, and they were on an espionage mission for the Warsaw Pact: to assess the security measures and the vulnerabilities of Western Europe's northern ports. It was Leonid

Brezhnev's dream to launch a surprise sweep across Western Europe and this mission was one of many to gather the necessary intelligence. But the skipper of the *Legya* was horrified by the nuclear retaliation that he knew would be unleashed upon his beloved Poland, should such a sweep occur.

The skipper's name was Ryszard Kuklinski; he was the Polish General Staff's liaison to the Warsaw Pact in Moscow, and once his crew was safely ashore he wrote and posted a letter to the American ambassador in Bonn, volunteering his services.

He spoke very little English, and at first his letter was dismissed as a clumsy attempt by some low-level Polish seaman to earn a few dollars as an intelligence peddler. But as CIA began to connect the dots, it took a second look. The *Legya*; was known to belong to the Polish General Staff, and even a low-level swabbie aboard such a vessel might indeed have an opportunity to pick up interesting bits of intelligence. More significantly, the man hadn't asked for or even hinted at money. And he had suggested potential meeting sites and times in Hamburg, Amsterdam and Antwerp, thereby displaying a knowledge of routes and schedules that an ordinary seaman would be unlikely to possess.

The Amsterdam Station was ordered to make contact, but to exercise particular care in case it was a provocation – or worse, an attempt to kidnap an American Intelligence officer. The case was code-named GULL.

Over the course of the next nine years GULL employed an array of TSD-produced devices to keep us abreast of Brezhnev's war plans, ultimately allowing President Carter to confront the Chairman via back channels and let him know that we had detailed knowledge of his plans. The Chairman backed off, and once again -- because the element of surprise had been short-circuited -- a dangerous escalation was avoided.

By 1981, however, it had become too risky for GULL to continue. The Polish security forces were conducting intensive security checks on the few who had access to the secrets that were being compromised, and it was just a matter of time before GULL would be caught.

The American Embassy's van made weekly trips from Warsaw to Berlin for supplies and the driver and his helper were well known to the border authorities. They were well liked, too, for they often did small favors for the guards: they brought back cigarettes and liquor from the PX and Class

VI stores, as well as girlie magazines and contraband that could be peddled on the black market. The guards could not legally inspect the van because of its diplomatic immunity, but they could and did use heat detectors and dogs to locate hidden bodies or possible defectors. Should their suspicions be aroused, they could forbid the vehicle to leave the country; at worst they might even violate diplomatic immunity and search it.

GULL was wrapped in thermal blankets to suppress heat emanations, and at the border the driver tossed the remains of his hamburger to the watchdog. The hamburger had been laced with an odorless chemical that temporarily deadened the animal's sense of smell, and Kuklinski was safely spirited out of the country. His wife and two sons were also exfiltrated successfully.

GULL died in his adopted home state of Washington in February, 2004. Newspapers on the West Coast and in Washington, DC carried his obituary, and NPR's *All Things Considered* devoted a poignant segment of its broadcast to the contributions of this quiet hero[11].

✷✷✷

TOLKACHEV:

On a dismal Moscow evening in January, 1977 a middle-aged man loitered over a glass of tea, across the street from a gas station frequented by diplomats. When a car he recognized from previous reconnaissance pulled up to a pump, he crossed the street and approached the driver.

"You are an American, yes?" The driver nodded. The Russian pushed a slip of paper through the window and shuffled off.

The note was short and specific. It said the writer had matters of importance to discuss with an American official. He suggested a time and two possible locations for the meeting: the driver was to park his car pointing in one direction if he wished to use the first, or in the opposite direction if he preferred the second of the two suggested sites.

But the Americans weren't buying; we didn't know the Russian's name, his position or what it was that he wanted to discuss. Once again Headquarters suspected that this was a provocation designed to flush out and identify CIA officers at the American embassy.

The Russian didn't give up. Again and again he approached Americans and each time revealed a little more about the material to which he had access. He was an engineer; he worked on advanced military avionics. Eventually he identified himself fully and provided eleven pages of detailed notes about one of the weapons systems the Soviets were developing.

The Air Force was ecstatic; if he could provide details on this work, it could save the United States five years or more of Research & Development time. That finally tipped the balance, and Headquarters authorized Moscow Station to proceed. The first meeting took place in August of 1978 -- a full 19 months after the agent's initial approach.

But if CIA was slow off the mark, it quickly made up for lost time. Over the course of the next few months the agent was provided with TSD-produced miniature cameras, secret writing materials, concealment devices and forged identity documents. The Office of Communications provided him with code pads and with a tiny device that could send and receive encrypted messages in a fraction of a second – too brief to be intercepted by the Soviets. Tolkachev preferred to do his clandestine photography at home, but could not leave the building without showing his building pass. At the same time he could not check out classified documents from the Files Section without leaving his building pass as security We duplicated his building pass to the last detail, and he was able to solve that problem.

Customer satisfaction with Tolkachev's reporting grew ever higher, and as a result of his information, the Air Force completely reversed its direction on a multi-million dollar electronics package for one of its latest fighter aircraft.

The primary value of the source's reporting was that it provided detailed data on new Soviet weapon systems that would not be available from technical collection sources for many years, if ever. The complete documentation on these systems, which the agent provided even before the systems were fully operational, was described as being of "incalculable value."[12]

For nine years this extraordinarily productive source gave the United States a ringside seat on the Soviet's development of advanced weapons systems. But in June of 1985 it ended, and in September of that year TASS carried a brief report that one A. L. Tolkachev, an engineer, had been convicted and executed for conspiring with the Americans.

Where did it go wrong?

In June 1983 the CIA had hired a bright and personable young man named Edward Lee Howard. He had served with distinction in the Peace Corps, and CIA began to train him for assignment to Moscow Station. As a part of his preparation he was read in on a number of Moscow Station's operations, including the Tolkachev case.

Shortly before his scheduled departure date, however, CIA began to suspect Howard of petty thievery: small, personal items had disappeared from colleagues' desks; expense vouchers he submitted didn't tally. He was polygraphed again (subjected to a lie detector test) and failed, and shortly thereafter he was fired.

Howard was not a happy camper. He became a binge drinker and ultimately a full-scale alcoholic. In late 1984 he flew to Vienna, contacted the Soviet embassy and volunteered his services to the KGB. One of the many agents he compromised was Adolf Tolkachev, and his reporting was confirmed by a second KGB agent – Aldrich Ames.

Howard fled to the Soviet Union, where a few months later he was killed in an accidental fall. Aldrich Ames is serving a life sentence in a Federal penitentiary, without the possibility of parole.

***

These cases underscore a trenchant point: When it came to actual re-cruitments, CIA recruited few Soviet agents of real significance. I thought that this just reflected my own ignorance and that surely there were operations to which I was not privy that were more successful. But that assertion has been echoed by Paul Redmond[13], retired chief of CIA's Soviet Division, and by the memoirs of a former Director of Central Intelligence, Adm. Stansfield Turner.

The KGB's Maj. Gen. Oleg Kalugin, maintains that the Soviets were not a great deal more successful than were we; this was substantially their experience as well. [In order to not embarrass his hosts, I suspect Gen. Kalugin is being a bit too modest and self-effacing; Jay Epstein's definitive article in the Sept. 28th issue of the New York Times magazine[14] lists an impressive number of high-level penetrations of Western services by the KGB].

The agents that provided some of the most critical intelligence to both sides, however, were the Walk-Ins – those individuals who, for their own reasons, made the initial approach and themselves volunteered to work for the other side: Kim Philby, George Blake, Edward Lee Howard and Aldrich Ames for the Soviets, Oleg Penkovsky, Ryszard Kuklinsky, and Adolf Tolkachev to name but a few for the Americans. There were more, but they all had one characteristic in common: the Intelligence Services did not recruit *them*; it was *they* who made the initial approaches.

***

Much of our work was quite prosaic, though often it led to technical advances from which the public benefited:

We needed a small surveillance camera for street use that could be operated from within a concealment device. This meant that the camera had to adjust *itself*, automatically for focus and light conditions. The R&D we funded made it the precursor to today's 'aim & shoot' cameras.

We spent enormous sums and endangered many agents' lives to emplace audio and video devices, along with other sensors, deep inside denied areas. Too often they would fail because of the inherent unreliability of the only batteries then in existence – the old carbon/zinc cells that used to leak all over our flashlights. The big battery manufacturers had little interest in making reliable batteries, for the faster they failed the more they sold.

As electronic circuitry shrank in size, the clunky old batteries that powered them became the largest part of the systems. The first step forward was our development of the tiny silver cell – which ultimately came to power pacemakers as well. We also came across a garage shop operation that was experimenting with lithium, and gave them a sack full of money. Within 18 months our battery problems began to diminish, and it is the successors to those lithium cells that power most of today's watches, cameras and cell phones.

The Vanessa project, described earlier, that played a role in the Church Committee's investigation of CIA, required the development of a slightly sticky sheet of paper that could be pressed up against a surface – in Vanessa's case to remove particulate matter. That 'slightly sticky sheet' is now a common, household item.

Finally (and quite unexpectedly), a TSD camera was the first to reach the moon. It wasn't supposed to be. We didn't mean it to be, but here is how it came about:

Compared to the 'big boys' -- NASA and Defense – TSD's R&D budget was miniscule, and our ability to have contractors assign their very best scientists and engineers to our requirements was paltry indeed. We badly wanted a low-light video camera, at a time when such things did not exist, but acquiring the funds or commanding the talent to create one, was well beyond our reach.

Then fortune smiled upon us: NASA needed a low-light video camera for Apollo II, which was to land on the dark side of the moon. They engaged a major defense contractor and shelled out enormous sums to produce six such devices, while we gnashed our teeth, and salivated. But half way through their development, a second contractor persuaded NASA that it had a better design, and NASA summarily switched gears

We came, hat in hand, groveled appropriately, and NASA magnanimously 'allowed us' to pick up the bill for the little work that remained on the original design. In due course we became the proud owners of six low-light video cameras, each about the size of a loaf of Pepperidge Farms bread.

Unfortunately, the second contractor did not complete his development by launch date. NASA came to us, hat in hand, groveled appropriately, and we magnanimously 'gave them' two of our low-light video cameras. It made our day!

And it was one of those cameras that broadcast Neil Armstrong's famous "One Small Step For Man..." to a jubilant world. He then, inadvertently, pointed the camera at the horizon's bright rim – which totally overwhelmed the unit's low-light element, and burned it out. But it had done its job.

***

And then I blew it.

As Dr. Gottlieb's EXO, I had the dubious privilege of setting up PR-presentations. One day the Director of Central Intelligence announced that he had invited the entire Senate's Subcommittee on Intelligence to a dinner briefing in the DCI's dining room. He wanted to include a Show & Tell of some of TSD's more awesome goodies. I was ordered to assemble a suitable selection.

Conventional dead drops – innocuous objects such as a discarded can, a hollowed-out branch, or a modified brick that could conceal a few rolls of film – were of limited operational value; too often they would be picked up by an innocent scavenger, for in every society beset by shortages, someone's trash is someone else's treasure.

But no scavenger, however desperate, is likely to be attracted to an emaciated and flea-bitten, dead rat. We had a taxidermist prepare several for us, and equipped their bellies with a cleverly concealed zipper. They could hold money, rolls of film, communications devices or other clandestine objects.

I decided to include a rat in our display, and while the guests were having cocktails in the DCI's conference room, set up the exhibits in the dining room. Of course, no one wants to have dinner under the baleful eye of an eviscerated rat, and I carefully covered that exhibit with a napkin before departing. A few moments later the chief steward came in to check the room and to make sure that all was in order. He picked up a napkin some careless waiter had left behind and discovered (Ohmygawd!) a dead rat in the DCI's dining room. He fetched a pair of tongs, and dropped the offending animal down the incinerator chute.

Unfortunately he left the napkin behind, and when the DCI whisked it away with a great flourish to present the exhibit's *pièce de resistance* -- there was nothing but an empty plate.

I was never asked to set up another exhibit for the DCI.

✻✻✻

A PERSONAL PERSPECTIVE

While the 9/11 Commission's Report highlighted some distinct weaknesses, three major impediments to America's approach to Intelligence were not addressed. All, in my opinion, were crucial contributors to the 9/11 failures, and none will be affected by legislation or organizational changes.

The first of these is America's antipathy to the intelligence process. It offends the core values of a democratic society, and however jaundiced we may pretend to be, they are values we hold dear. The secrecy. The chicanery. The CIA's well-publicized complicity in the overthrow of democratically elected governments, the Abu Ghraib scandal, the Vice President's stolid attempts to allow a torture exception for the CIA, and now the revelation of widespread wiretapping without court sanction. As a people, such tactics make us very uncomfortable. However justifiable the ends, we abhor the means.

Although few professions can match it in terms of breadth, exposure and personal satisfaction, too many of us discourage our bright and gifted children from pursuing Intelligence as a career, and the nation is the poorer for it. That is one casualty of our antipathy to the Intelligence process, but there is a far more serious one:

We tolerate the intelligence process in times of crisis, but we shut it down the moment the crisis has passed. That has been our practice since the end of World War I, when Secretary of State Henry Stimson drove the final nail into the coffin by declaring that "Gentlemen do not read other people's mail." It was an attitude that contributed to our lack of human sources on Japan's Imperial Staff, and was a major reason we were caught flat-footed by the Japanese attack on Pearl Harbor.

You would think that we would have learned our lesson, but we did the same after World War II, when we dismantled the OSS. And again after the Cold War, when we closed down our agent networks in Afghanistan. And yet a fourth time after the first Gulf War, when we walked away from our agent networks in Iraq. As a result, we had few human sources to warn us about the attacks on the Khobar Towers in Saudi Arabia, on the USS Cole, in Yemen, on the bombings of our embassies in Nairobi and Dar es Salaam, and of course on the 9/11 attack itself.

Who is responsible for this short-sightedness? It is we, the people who are responsible. We have an aging infrastructure that badly needs repair. Schools that need to be built. Ports that need to be secured, and a healthcare system spiraling out of control.

God forbid that we should raise taxes to pay for the things we need. So we tell our legislators: "Hey, the Kaiser is dead. Hitler's gone. The Soviet Union is toast. So how come you're still funding all them spies?" And legislators and presidents listen, because they like being re-elected.

Each time we dismantle our Intelligence capabilities, the experienced hands melt away. Their education, their language skills, and their intimate knowledge of foreign leaders make them very attractive to the private sector, and they get good jobs elsewhere. As veteran New York Times reporter James Risen observed:

"Over a three or four year period in the early to mid-1990's, virtually an entire generation of CIA officers – the people who had won the Cold War – quit or retired. One CIA veteran compared the agency to an airline that had lost all of its senior pilots."[15]

While a given crisis may be weathered, the challenges to our security don't really disappear; they merely go dormant -- or change their spots. Yesterday's military adversaries morph into today's economic and ideological ones, and the mass departure of our 'senior pilots' has made it that much more difficult to adapt. Thus we hastily embark upon a new round of recruitments, pick up greenhorns like me from the corner of 32nd & Ploughed Ground, and train them to be spies. It's a development process that, as Director George Tenet observed, takes 5 – 10 years, and in the meantime we function at sub-professional levels.

The American public's antipathy to the Intelligence process makes it an attractive target for budget cuts. It has no constituency; a government perennially short of funds would rather use the money elsewhere. The public's antipathy is an <u>attitudinal</u> impediment; it is probably a permanent impediment, and will be unaffected by organizational changes.

The second impediment is bias. We tend to forget that the Intelligence process, *by design*, casts as wide net as possible and collects evidence on <u>all</u> sides of an issue. Inevitably there will be data that support one point of view, and other reporting that supports the opposite. A professional service tries to weigh both with objectivity.

Total objectivity is rare and to a greater or lesser degree, bias and mind-set will often intrude on the process. We just can't believe that 'x' could be true, and we therefore discount any evidence to the contrary.

This is not a uniquely American problem: According to Efraim Halevey, former head of the Mossad, the Israelis were caught by surprise by the Yom Kippur War because they simply refused to believe that the Egyptians and Syrians had the ability (or the guts) to mount such an attack..

The entire world was surprised by the Hamas victory in Palestine's 2006 elections — as was Hamas itself, and in the summer of 2006 the vaunted Israeli service again blew it when it grossly underestimated Hezbollah's capacity and resilience. Indeed as these words are being written the Israeli Knesset is launching a major investigation into this apparent Intelligence failure.

Despite Adm. Canaris' reported warnings to the contrary, Hitler was so convinced that the United States would remain neutral, that he launched his attack on Western Europe with impunity. "You'll see," he is said to have assured his Intelligence Chief, "the Isolationists will prevail. They dislike the Jews as much as we do." He was not entirely wrong; we *did* stay out of the war for over two years — until the Japanese attacked us at Pearl Harbor.

Finally, President Johnson was so convinced that Hanoi had tried to torpedo one of our ships in the Tonkin Gulf (a conclusion not shared by the Navy), and was so concerned that Sen. Barry Goldwater would label him 'soft on Communism,' that he muscled the Tonkin Gulf Resolution through Congress and catapulted us into the Vietnam War.[16]

Bias is a common human failing, and Saddam Hussein's reported Weapons of Mass Destruction were only one more example. Sure, Hussein had once had an active WMD program, and his refusal to allow the UN's weapons inspectors to do their job lent fuel to the idea that he had them still. But as we are learning to an ever greater extent, there was little hard evidence to support it.

Bias is bad enough when displayed by professionals; it is infinitely worse when it stems from political agendas and is imposed from above. When the data point 80/20 or 70/30 toward one conclusion, externally-imposed bias is easier to resist, but the closer the evidence approaches a 50/50 split, the more likely it is that bias will intrude. And with political appointees (instead of professionals) heading an agency, an Administration's bias is going to influence the product, regardless of whether it is a Republican or a Democrat occupying the White House.

In a recent article in *Foreign Affairs*, CIA's Counter-Terrorism chief Paul Pillar writes that no Administration officials tried to pressure his analysts to <u>change</u> their reports; instead those officials simply *ignored* the reporting that did not support the Administration's bias. Former National Security Advisor Richard A. Clark makes essentially the same charge, as does retired 4-Star Gen. Anthony Zinny, former commander of CENTCOM, in his new book, *'Battle for Peace'*. In an interview on Meet the Press on April 2nd, 2006, Gen Zinny quotes VP Cheney:

> "Simply stated, there is no doubt now that Sadam Hussein has weapons of mass destruction; there is no doubt that he is amassing them to use against our friends, against our allies and against us."

Zinny goes on to say, "I did consulting work for CIA right up to the beginning of the war. I watched the intelligence, and *never, not once*, did it say that he has WMDs. I never saw anything. I'd say to the analysts 'Where's the threat?' Their response was silence".

Zinny's conclusion, as Cheney pressed on, was the same as that of National Security Advisor Richard A. Clark and Secretary of the Treasury Paul O'Neal: that the Bush administration was determined to go to war. Moments later he had an even more chilling thought: "These guys don't understand what they're getting into."

Bias is the second impediment to the Intelligence process; it is a human failing from which most of us suffer, but is infinitely more dangerous when driven by political agendas. It too cannot be remedied by legislation.

Contempt is the third. Throughout the Cold War we benefited greatly from cooperation with the Intelligence services of other nations, and sometimes even made common cause with nations that were supposedly our enemies. While political leaders on both sides were fulminating and posturing (usually for internal consumption), we were quietly able to relate, professional to professional, when it was in our mutual interest to do so

Because of proximity, language, tribal relationships, or common borders, they often had access to information that we did not. They had human sources on the ground with the ethnic backgrounds, local knowledge and language skills that we could not hope to match. In exchange, we could supply technical intelligence of enormous value, and surveillance capabilities far more advanced than theirs. In short, we could trade -- and trade we did.

Iraq is a good example: It is likely that the Syrians and the Iranians had far better intelligence on Hussein's weapons of mass destruction than did we — he was certainly more of a threat to them than he was to us. But theirs are proud and ancient civilizations, and when we ridicule them, humiliate them publicly, and label them as the "Axis of Evil" can we really expect any help from them? When we contemptuously dismiss all of our Western European allies as 'Old Europe' and (good grief!) reclassify French Fries as Freedom Fries, are they likely to cooperate with us?

I'm happy to see that the Administration is once again starting to recognize the value of liaison relationships, but I suspect that its open contempt of sister services played a role in the 9/11 fiasco as well.

Antipathy, Bias and Contempt -- the ABC's of intelligence failure that cannot be rectified by legislation. As Pogo put it: "We has met the enemy, and he is us."

***

Martha tolerated lithium carbonate well, and regained much of her old fire. She got a job on Capitol Hill, on Senator Paul Sarbane's staff, and became the 'Mother Confessor' and 'Ann Landers' to the bright and bushytailed young girls in his office. And then one day we discovered a lump, which led to a mastectomy -- and a long, harsh bout of chemotherapy.

It was a wake-up call. If we were going to do any serious sailing, it would have to be sooner if it was going to be at all. When she completed her chemotherapy we spent a year choosing and outfitting a sturdy 37' sloop, and in 1980 I took advantage of the generous, early retirement benefits allowed Clandestine Services officers. Adm. Stansfield Turner patted me on the head, awarded me a medal for activities he preferred not to specify, and we embarked upon the next chapter of our lives. I had just turned 52.

***

4

THE SAILING YEARS

I have always been mesmerized by the sea. I love its undulations and its ever-changing moods. It is capricious, playful, and contemptuous of error. It is vicious one moment, and benign the next. It challenges, probes for weaknesses, and takes advantage of every mistake. The sea wants you to acknowledge that it could crush you at any time -- without a moment's hesitation or remorse; it expects you to pay homage to its power. You don't fight the sea; you adapt to its temper. It is never at rest

Our sailing vessel, the *Mirage* was built for the sea. Actually, she was built for the bareboat charters trade, which some will tell you is even more challenging. It serves the hordes that flock to the South Atlantic, pretending to a greater knowledge of seamanship than they actually possess. They pass a brief qualifying test, take command of fiberglass juggernauts that displace 10 to 20 tons, bash into other juggernauts, or run them up on coral reefs. It is a maxim that a vessel that can survive a charter season can survive just about anything. The *Mirage* was in that category.

She was a CSY-37 -- a class financed by Jack Van Ost, a NJ Dentist who had chartered stock boats for years, and had seen how shoddily they were constructed. He hired a top-notch small boat architect named Peter Schmitt who designed a vessel that could meet the challenges of the charter trade. Her hull was of solid fiberglass, in places over 2" thick, and she carried 8,000 lbs of lead in her keel. Her stanchions were solid, 1" stainless steel rods – not tubing, as one finds on most stock boats. They were threaded at one end, and ran right through the cap-rail and into nuts and backing plates deeply embedded in the hull. The CSY-37 could be run up on a coral reef, could withstand being pounded by the sea until help arrived, and suffer only cosmetic damage. A heavy boat, designed for cruising rather than for racing, she was in her element in the Virgins, where the Trades so often blow at 25 knots or more.

We had only one serious criticism of the **Mirage**: her waste treatment system didn't work very well. Not a part of the original design, it was a last-minute add-on, made necessary by recently enacted environmental regulations, and we had to come up with another $2,000 to make the boat compliant. Instead of simply pumping our waste overboard, it now had to pass it through a processing chamber – a kind of septic tank that broke it down through bacterial action.

But it didn't work. It was a brand new design and the bugs (so to speak) had not yet been worked out. The damned thing clogged, or the bacteria didn't like the motion of the ocean and went on strike – whatever the explanation, there was a pervasive odor of drains about the boat, and at the first opportunity we bypassed the chamber and went back to pumping overboard.

When our son, Scott, then a medical student, heard what we had done, he became very angry with us: "Of all the advances that have been made in medicine," he said, "none have had as much impact on world health as sanitation. *Please* hook that system up again."

We tried; we really did, but to no avail. The processing chamber was right under our bunk, and the effect was like sleeping in an outhouse. Besides, these were environmental regulations that applied only to the United States — and we were heading for the Bahamas.

***

"Be not the first by whom the new are tried. . . ." was Alexander Pope's sage advice, but Walter Cronkite, the former CBS news anchor, ignored it. He bought the first of the CSY-37s and apparently it damn-near killed him. The shipyard had not yet gotten the hang of this new-fangled vessel, and reportedly, miles offshore in the Atlantic, Cronkite's propeller shaft suddenly uncoupled from the engine and the whole assembly slid out of the boat. Sea water rushed into the gaping hole, and only very quick thinking saved him and his vessel. That's the sea for you: it lurks and bides its time, then strikes when it finds a chink in the armor.

We also took delivery of our boat at CSY's yard in St. Petersburg, but it was hull #6, and by then the major errors had been corrected. We sailed around the southern tip of Florida, and piggy-backed the powerful Gulf Stream for the sleigh-ride north. The Stream is literally a river of hot water, ten times the volume of the Mississippi. It flows north, in spots adding as much as five knots to your speed. It hugs the East Coast as far as Cape Hatteras, then veers due East to warm Bermuda before heading for Cornwall and northern Europe. The waters of the North Atlantic can be gray and cold, but in the Gulf Stream they are a sapphire blue.

Cape Hatteras, though, is treacherous — a graveyard for small vessels. Shoals extend outward for miles, and when the warm waters of the Stream butt up against the cold currents coming down from Labrador, fog and other unpleasant conditions result, We were too inexperienced to risk a trip around Hatteras, and ducked inside to the Intra-Coastal Waterway, then into Chesapeake Bay and up the Potomac toward Washington. And there our adventure almost ended.

In many places the broad Potomac River is extremely shallow. For 90 miles it meanders through Virginia, often doubling back upon itself. A narrow channel allows for deeper draft vessels, but venture beyond its confines and you're likely to run aground.

We had wanted to reach Washington by a certain time, and were already a day behind schedule. The weather was good, the wind fair and though we were both exhausted, I persuaded Martha that we should sail on through the night. "It's nothing but a placid river," I assured her. "Piece of cake."

That was my first mistake: you don't take the sea or its tributaries for granted. Ever.

At around 2:00 AM we were making very good progress, gliding gently through a pastoral countryside. The wind was light and abaft our beam, but with our spinnaker boomed out we were making a steady three or four knots against the current, under a canopy of velvet, studded with diamonds. There was little to be seen or heard on shore: in the distance, a traffic light; here and there a barking dog. The sibilant whisper of the bow slicing through the water, and the gentle motion of the boat all contributed to euphoric inattention.

That was mistake #2. You never drop your guard. Not ever.

Only — and this was ridiculous, of course -- the traffic light I had seen seemed to be moving. A few moments earlier, it had been green and was well to our left. Now it had shifted; it was almost dead ahead, and a red light appeared -- not above it, but next to it.

What I had thought was a traffic light on shore, was in fact the starboard light of a huge barge assembly slowly snaking its way downstream. It had worked its way around one of the Potomac's giant loops, and suddenly it was dead ahead.

A brilliant spotlight cut through the darkness and blinded me. I threw the wheel hard over, praying that I had headed in the right direction, and promptly ran aground. Moments later a heavily laden barge slid by our port side, then a second and then a third. Finally the tug pushing this whole assembly came abreast and its skipper had a few uncomplimentary remarks he wanted to get off his chest.

Martha slept through the whole thing, and I didn't feel it necessary to burden her with a lot of detail; her confidence in me as a skipper had already been shaken: These were the days before GPSs and other electronic positioning systems. When out of sight of land, as we often would be, the only way to fix our position would be through celestial navigation. That required a good sextant, up to date celestial charts and sight-reduction tables, a great deal of patience -- and *lots* of practice.

A few weeks earlier I had practiced diligently from the highest point in Washington, did the tedious calculations and plotted Washington's exact location. In doing so I stumbled across the Cold War's best kept secret, meant to confuse Soviet missiles: Washington DC was actually located just five miles East of Denver, CO. Instead of applauding my discovery, Martha had gone off, shaking her head. I don't think she was really all that fond of Denver.

We had made a bargain: If she didn't like the sailing life after six months, we would swallow the anchor and return to Washington; we in fact did not put our house on the market for that reason.

Five months later it looked like the string was running out: she missed her friends and she missed the stimulation of Capitol Hill. But then our daughter, Saissy, joined us for a month, along with our niece, Tilda, and her reservations melted. For the next three and a half years we lived aboard, spending most of our time in the Bahamas, only returning to Miami to re-provision and for Martha's periodic cancer check-ups.

The Bahamas consist of over 700 islands and 2,000 cays, scattered across a basin almost the size of Texas. Fewer than three dozen of these islands are settled, and most are less than a square mile in size. It makes for many snug anchorages.

They are in fact just the highpoints of what was once an enormous land mass, until melting glaciers raised the level of the oceans. The flooded area (called the Bahamas Bank) is not very far below the surface; its average depth is just 15 feet, and it is studded with a minefield of coral heads that are often only four or five feet below the surface. When the sun is over your shoulder, these heads are clearly visible, for the waters are incredibly clear. But their locations are not charted, and prior to the advent of affordable GPS systems, only the locals (and the very foolish) would attempt to cross the Bank at night.

The Bahamian Defense Force had two ancient cutters with which to police that enormous area. Attempting to collect taxes from the few settlements spread across its territories would have been an impossible task, and they didn't even try. Instead, the Bahamian government imposed a very high tariff on all goods brought into the country, and as the Bahamas have no industry, and the shallowness of the soil will not support commercial farming, that included just about everything. We caught and cooked a lot of fish, baked our own bread, bought milk and vegetables from the local farmers' markets, but went back to Miami every three months to re-provision.

That meant crossing the Gulf Stream, and in a slow-moving sailboat that is always a challenge. The Florida Straits that separate the Bahamas from the United States are only 50 miles wide, and as the northward-flowing Stream is compressed to pass through this 'narrow' opening, its current increases to four or five knots at the center.

The prevailing winds are from the East, and when they shift South of East, the Stream can be quite docile: wind and current are flowing in more or less the same direction. But when the wind shifts North of East, the wind flow opposes the current, and the Stream can become very ugly, creating choppy waves of 15 to 20 feet or more in height. Time and again holiday makers on a tight schedule would leave Florida for the Bahamas when the winds were from the Northern quadrants, and would return a few hours later with broken spars and serious injuries. We often had to lie at anchor for a week or more, waiting for the winds to shift to a favorable quarter, but we didn't care; we weren't on a schedule.

At midnight one June evening we hoisted anchor and set out from Marathon Florida. Our destination: Gun Cay, about 14 hours away. The winds were from the Southeast at 12 knots and the forecast was for fair weather.

Good news, for between Gun and Cat Cays, the entrance to the Great Bahamas Bank is tricky. Right on its western edge, the entrance is protected by a coral reef that parallels the shore and creates a channel about 150 yards wide. You sail due East toward a lighthouse on Gun Cay, turn South into the channel between the reef and the Cay to run close to the shore, then turn Northeast again to pass through a narrow entrance to the Bahamas Bank.

But you're not home free. Dead ahead a large sandbar blocks access to the Bank and you must turn to the North to clear it. Only then can you breathe easy -- and crawl exhausted into your bunk.

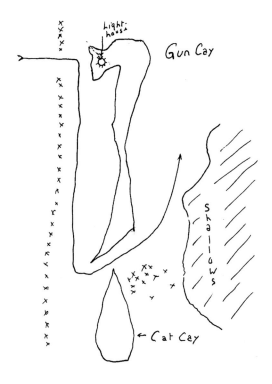

The passage was an easy one, and by 1:30 the next afternoon we were within a few miles of the reef – the xxx's in the picture. I could see the lighthouse plainly and positioned ourselves so that we would pass safely through the cut in the reef, on a course of 90 degrees. But the sky was turning a coppery color, and behind us the clouds were an angry black. Suddenly the wind whipped around to the Northwest, increased to gale force, and like an express train we were carried toward the reefs. Then the rain came down in sheets, and we could no longer see the lighthouse that marked the location of the cut.

We were sailing blind, now, just praying that we were still headed squarely for the cut. And luck was with us. Once safely through the reef, we turned South, ran the 500 yards parallel to the shore and turned Northeast again to pass safely through the entrance.

We still had to avoid the sandbar, however – the shoals to the right of the entrance -- but turning North to do so put us too close to the wind. I turned on the ignition to start the engine, and it wouldn't catch. Again, and still the engine wouldn't start. The sails shuddered; the boat slowed, came to a stop, and then gradually gathered speed in reverse as the wind forced us back toward the opening.

I rushed forward, threw out the anchor and hoped that it would grab. It didn't; the bottom was hard limestone and there was no place for the anchor to dig in. But at the last moment, miraculously, a fluke caught on a rock or crevasse, the ¾" nylon anchor line stretched like a rubber band as it took the strain of a 20,000 lb vessel moving backwards at about a knot, and the *Mirage* abruptly came to a stop. We were sitting squarely across the opening, denying entrance to any other vessel, but we hoped that no other boat would be out sailing in that weather.

The engine had failed to start because the fuel line was clogged. Somewhere we had taken on contaminated diesel, and sediment had gotten past our fuel filters. It took less than thirty minutes to clear the fuel line, and then we were able to motor into calm waters in the lee of Gun Cay – to fortify ourselves with a stiff drink.

Our destination on his trip was Nassau, but first we had to cross the Bahamas Bank – 70 miles wide. You have the entire Bank to yourself; you station your crew forward, to watch for coral heads, and you're tempted to shed the clothes and fully enjoy the sun.

But don't leave 'em below. The moment the bathing suits come off, an Orion aircraft is sure to appear overhead, scouring the Bank for drug runners. And the frantic attempts on deck to cover up, are the principal sources of amusement for the crew.

There is just one man-made structure on that 70 mile wide bank – the long-abandoned Russell Beacon, erected years go for aircraft guidance. Once a monument to a great technical achievement, it is now just a mass of rusted metal. You are reminded immediately of Shelley's poem that described what remains of a once-great statue to the emperor Ozymandias. It concludes:

"*. . .and on the pedestal, these words appear:*
'My Name is Ozymandias, King of Kings.
Look on my works, ye Mighty, and despair!'

"Nothing beside remains.
Around the ruins of that colossal wreck,
The lone and level sands stretch far and wide."

***

Years later Sharon and I left Miami at 10:00 PM, on another crossing of the Gulf Stream – this time bound for West End, the northern-most point of the Bahamas. The islands there are very low -- just a few feet above sea-level, and if we miscalculated and missed them, we'd either end up on the ubiquitous reefs that surround the Bahamas Bank -- or our next stop would be Europe.

And without the benefit of today's electronic navigation devices, that was more than a slight risk: we would be sailing into the sunrise; the low-lying land would be in silhouette – hardly visible at all.

West End, however, had a tall, though very skinny, radio mast, with a flashing red light. On a clear night it was visible for 20 miles or more. If we could spot that light before the sun rose, we could correct for any errors that the north-flowing Gulf Stream might have introduced. Here, too, the entrance was guarded by reefs, but two sticks were said to mark the edges of the cut.

That is, (or was then), very typical of the Bahamas. A third-world country, it scraped up the money for proper buoys at its major ports, but most cuts through the reefs that surrounded the country were simply marked by pushing branches into cracks in the coral. Sometimes storms washed them away; sometimes the locals deliberately removed them in the hopes of creating wrecks that they could salvage.

It all went as planned; we spotted the flashing red light, made our course corrections and at about 6:00 AM the depth sounder reported that the bottom was starting to shoal. We were approaching the reef, but there weren't *two* sticks marking the edges of the cut; there was only one. Did it mark the left edge of the cut or the right? Should we pass it to port, or take it to starboard? The sun was right in our eyes and we couldn't 'read' the water.

We crept forward, gambling that we should pass to the left of the branch (i.e., 'take the marker to starboard'). If we grounded, it would be lightly and we could back off. But the seas were choppy and while the CSY-37 had a reputation for being able to tolerate it, we didn't relish the prospect of being bounced up and down on a coral reef for a few hours. At the very last moment I got cold feet, turned the boat around and headed out to think about it some more.

The safer course, obviously, would be to stand off and wait for a local fishing trawler to come out of the cut, thereby marking the channel, but we were tired, and the wind was beginning to strengthen and to veer to the north; pretty soon the Gulf Stream would become ugly.

Taking the marker to port was probably the better choice, and we started to do so. But just then a school of dolphin swept by our bow, playfully leaping and cavorting about before heading onto the Bahamas Bank for breakfast. They took the marker to starboard; that's where the deeper water lay. Dumb luck -- but our first choice had been the correct one after all. We followed them in and anchored safely on the Bank for a breakfast of our own.

***

"MAYDAY, MAYDAY, MAYDAY!" I had the radio's volume turned down low as I worked at the chart table, but turned it up as I listened for the Coast Guard's response. MAYDAY is the international distress call, a bastardization of the French phrase, *M'aidez.* – Help me! The signal was weak, and the woman calling sounded at the end of her tether. But the Coast Guard didn't respond. "MAYDAY, MAYDAY, MAYDAY. This is the Sailing Vessel *Lucinda.*" The call came again, this time more urgently.

Amateur ('Ham') Radio was our principal means of communications, and while transmissions could travel thousands of miles, atmospherics, sun spots, time of day and the frequency all affected where they could be heard. Obviously her signal was skipping over and was not being heard by Coast Guard Norfolk.

"This is November 3, Delta, Delta Romeo," I finally replied, giving our call sign; "the Sailing Vessel *Mirage.* Can we help?"

"N3DDR, this is the S/V *Lucinda*, and we're in trouble. We are returning from the Dutch West Indies via the Yucatan Channel and because of storms we have been unable to get a celestial fix for the past three days.

I'm not at all sure where we are. Our engine failed, my husband fractured his right arm, and is doped up on pain pills. I've been trying to manage the boat by myself, but I'm just exhausted. And now I'm afraid of blundering into Cuban waters."

"*Lucinda,* let me try to raise Norfolk and relay for you," I said, and was able to do so. But the Gulf of Mexico is huge, and the Coast Guard was not willing to dispatch a Search & Rescue unit without a more precise location.

"Has she sighted any shipping within the past few hours," Norfolk inquired?

She had. A large cruise ship, about three hours earlier. She had tried to raise the vessel on her VHF radio, she said, but they had not responded.

"Ask her whether she was able to notice any distinctive markings on the hull, or on the ship's stack?"

She had — she remembered a crimson stack with a large, crescent moon.

Norfolk was silent for a few moments. "Those are the markings of the Carnival Cruise Lines," Norfolk finally announced; "we're contacting them now to see what ships they had in her area." I relayed the news to *Lucinda.*

Fifteen minutes later Norfolk not only had the answer, but the cruise ship's exact location, three hours earlier. And by consulting current tables and meteorological data they were able to estimate how far the *Lucinda* would have sailed in the intervening time. It was close enough for the S&R team, and an Orion was dispatched from Homestead AFB in Florida to look for her.

She heard the plane's engines first, then it burst through the overcast. "Oh my God — he's beautiful," the woman sobbed, breaking down in tears. "You're beautiful, pilot. Can you hear me?"

"Yes m'am," the Orion responded, laconically. "Happy we could be of help."

Forty minutes later a helicopter was overhead. Two crew members were dropped to help the lady bring her vessel into Key West, and to minister to her husband. When rescued, *Lucinda* was fourteen miles outside of Cuba's territorial waters.

***

The Exumas are a string of small islands, a hundred miles long, running north and south. They form a barrier against the heavy Atlantic swells, but are not high enough to block the ocean winds that sweep across them and on to the Bahamas Bank. They are popular not only because of the superb, protected sailing they provide, but because one of those islands -- Staniel Cay – is where a portion of the James Bond movie, *Thunderball* was filmed.

An large, hollow rock, about a half mile offshore, is in fact a cave in which a portion of that movie was filmed. Its only entrance is 4 feet under-water and is often guarded by a nurse shark. The 7' creature scares the hell out of you when you first see it, but nurse sharks have bony gums rather than teeth and, unless you argue with them over a fish you've speared, they ignore you. You dive down, swim through the entrance and surface again inside the cave. Little shafts of sunlight filter through cracks in the dome, the water is crystal clear, and the silence inside the cave is profound.

The whole area is a wildlife preserve and no fishing is allowed. Because of this the water in the cave is teeming with colorful fish and lobster – and that's what the nurse shark is waiting for: when one of them is foolish enough to venture outside the cave, it is unlikely to return.

A year had passed since our communication with the *Lucinda,* and we were anchored at Bell Island in the Exumas. We heard another call for help, and the exchange went something like this:

"This is the S/V *Good Times,* in the Atlantic, about two miles east of the Exumas. I'm having engine troubles. Can anyone lend assistance?" In the background I could hear a strident, female voice complaining: "I want to get off this Goddamned Boat, Fred!"

"*Good Times,* this is the *Mirage.* Where are you, exactly, and what's the problem?"

"Christ, *Mirage,* all these friggin' islands look alike. I think we're north of Staniel Cay, maybe ten, twelve miles. Our engine overheated; I think it's the water-pump." In the background I could hear: "Fred, tell the man I want to get off this boat RIGHT NOW!"

"*Good Times, Mirage.* Look for an island shaped like an inverted 'Y' There are several boats in the anchorage, and you may be able to spot our masts poking up above the treetops. It's a good, natural harbor, with an easy entrance. You should be able to sail right in, and drop the hook."

There was a long silence, though in the background we could hear the lady complaining, "Fred, you didn't tell the man.. ..." Finally Fred came back on the air: "Er.. we don't have sails rigged," he said. "And I wouldn't know how to work them if we did."

Fred was a commercial airline pilot who had purchased the boat and leased it back to a charter outfit. The lease-back contract had been completed, and Fred flew to the Bahamas to retrieve his vessel. Though he had never sailed before, he persuaded his girlfriend to come along, promising that they would motor leisurely to Nassau, then fly home from there. He would hire a crew to sail the vessel back to the United States.

"*Good Times, Mirage.* Drop an anchor and we'll tow you in. Among the boats in the anchorage we can probably find the parts needed to fix your water pump."

We motored out and spotted *Good Times* riding at anchor about a mile away. Fred was looking frazzled, his companion decidedly hostile. "I can't wait to get off this boat," she muttered, as we drew alongside and passed them a line. She insisted on coming aboard, plopped herself down in the cockpit, and sulked.

Another boat in the anchorage, *Le Moustache*, was getting ready to set sail, and I asked where they were headed.

"Just to Staniel", came the reply.

"There's a small airstrip on Staniel Cay," I said, "and this lady seems very anxious to get back to civilization. Could she possibly hitch a ride?"

Le Moustache was a 45' French beauty, with three couples aboard. The girls were gorgeous in their string bikinis, and Fred's companion wasn't going to pose any competition whatsoever. Sure, they agreed, she could come aboard.

The lady returned to *Good Times*, threw a few possessions into a duffle and transferred to the French vessel. Then anchor chains rattled, sails were hoisted and *Le Moustache* eased gracefully out of the harbor.

But as she departed, her crew stripped. Everything came off: guys and gals, sailing stark naked -- as the French so often do. And as she rounded the headland, the gentle breeze carried a plaintive wail across the water:

"GET ME OFF THIS BOAT!"

***

One evening we anchored at Little San Salvador Cay — a storybook tropical island with a white, crescent beach and coconut palms galore. One other sailboat was already at anchor, and we had this idyllic place to ourselves. But the following morning the cruise ship *Norway* pulled into the cove, dropped anchor, and disgorged a landing crew that set up tents, enormous grills and a Hawaiian combo. Then the 1,800 passengers were loaded into launches and brought ashore for games, limbo contests, snorkeling, ring tennis and barbecue. It was total pandemonium; the island was actually 'owned' by the Norwegian Line.

At 4:30 the ship's whistle blew, the passengers all returned to the launches and the clean-up crews came ashore and removed every trace of the visit. They even raked the beach. Not a cigarette butt, bottle cap or candy wrapper remained. Like the mythical *Brigadoon*, the island sank back into uninhabited obscurity.

We hailed their launch and apologized for having trespassed on their island, but they thanked us for having anchored there; passengers, they said, liked to see the sailboats; it gave them something to photograph. They offered us steaks, frozen orange juice concentrate and ice cream, but as the latter two only came in 5 gal. drums and wouldn't possibly fit in our little freezer, we just settled for the steaks.

A few months later we anchored at Warderick Wells. When I tried to raise the anchor the following morning I found that it had fouled on a wreck. We learned later that it had been a sailboat of about our size. The couple had rowed to shore to explore the island, and a few moments after they had shoved off in their dinghy, their boat blew up and burned to the waterline. They had had a leak in their propane tank, and as propane is heavier than air, it had settled in the bilges. When their automatic bilge pump had cycled on, the spark ignited the propane. They had their lives (and their dinghy), but they lost everything else.

***

We were on a re-provisioning run to Miami when our son Scott asked if he might borrow the boat for a week. An excellent sailor, he was as enthusiastic about the sport as we were, and also wanted to impress a new lady friend. The timing was perfect, for we were planning to fly to Washington to visit friends, and were happy to leave the boat in good hands.

When we returned we were greeted by a very happy Scott: "I'm so glad you took my advice and hooked the waste treatment system up again," he burbled, "even though it does make the stateroom somewhat fragrant."

Sure enough, it was Outhouse City all over again. Only this time the smell was not coming from the processing chamber. Scott's girl had tried to flush a sanitary pad down the toilet and it had jammed. Vigorous pumping simply burst the waste hose and from then on and for the rest of the week, all waste had piled up in the bilges. And as Scott and his girl had a plane to catch, guess who was left to clean out the mess.

On a subsequent re-provisioning trip, in 1984, we found that Martha's cancer had returned. We continued to live aboard for a few more months, commuting from our anchorage to her oncologist, but it became too difficult for her to manage. We bought a little condo in Miami and moved ashore.

***

Why this 'compulsion' to go sailing? Why this readiness to imprison oneself in a fiberglass box, at the mercy of the winds and the sea, for months at a time? It's a question sailors often ask one another and of course there are a zillion answers. But if there is any consensus, perhaps it is this: Most of our lives we are captives of forces and events we can only partially influence. To be sure, they usually result from choices that we ourselves have made — like the mortgage payments, or the demands of the profession we have chosen — but too often they are totally beyond our control: An employer moves his operation overseas, and we have to look for a new job. Or the president mobilizes the Reserves, and suddenly our orderly world is set on its ear. My career boiled down 30 years of mostly reacting to threats orchestrated by our enemies — real or imagined..

That was the appeal of cruising and blue-water sailing to us: We could go *where* we wanted and *when* we wanted to go. We would sink or survive on the basis of *our* skills, *our* preparations and *our* forethought. We didn't have the electronic positioning devices that are available today, and when we arrived at a destination more or less on schedule, it was a great rush — equal parts of pride, relief and gratitude. We had done everything right; the obstacles had been successfully overcome -- and a whimsical Nature had chosen not to squash us. True, there was always the chance that we might be capsized by a tidal wave or rammed by a whale, but those were such rare occurrences that we could safely ignore them.

Secondly, it was an extraordinarily healthy lifestyle and it was very inexpensive, too. Tending sails and diving the reefs for dinner kept us in beautiful shape, and for less than $12,000 a year (in 1980 dollars) we not only lived very comfortably, but could fly to see our children from time to time and even pay for their tickets to join us. .

For there was really nothing on which to spend money. We rarely put into marinas because there were so very few of them; our forty gallons of diesel fuel would last us at least two months; in a downpour we'd wait five minutes for the rain to wash the decks clean of salt residue, then flip a lever to route the run-off into our water tanks. Our two 20# propane bottles would handle our cooking and baking needs for three months; our little wind generator fed a steady 2 Amps of current back into our batteries, and by running the engine for just 30 minutes a day we kept the refrigerator cold, and warmed a separate fresh water tank for wash-ups and showers.

It was mind-boggling to tote up the amount of money we were spending ashore, even to live frugally. Mortgages, homeowners fees, utility bills, car payments, repairs, gas and insurance, clothing for all occasions, dues and membership fees, movie and theater tickets, cable TV charges, restaurant bills, ever escalating food bills -- and of course insidious impulse buying. It never ended.

In the early 1980's there were 300 or more sailors living aboard and cruising the area between Chesapeake Bay and the Virgin Islands, and that number I suspect has more than doubled since. To this day, the Waterway Net meets every morning at 7:30 via radio and exchanges tips on weather and anchorages, files float plans and helps with advice on mechanical problems. One radio operator is in charge, and if a sailor wants to ask a question, or make a comment or an announcement, he just gives his call sign. When his turn comes around, the operator calls on him to speak his piece. If two boats want to converse with each other, they make their initial contact on the Net, move to a different frequency to converse, and then return to the Net when done.

With so large a membership, if a sailor in the Bahamas needed to replace a heat-exchanger in his engine, there was sure to be another sailor just about to leave Miami who would buy it and bring it out to him. When we'd pull into a sheltered cove for the night, we'd often find several other boats already at anchor, and one or more would be couples that we had encountered before. We had no lack of companionship and interaction.

If we were to be asked for just one piece of advice by a potential live-aboard, it would be this: Choose the very largest boat you can afford -- and then buy one size larger. No matter how close you are to your companion, you will want your private space from time to time. You will want an area where you can work on engine parts of other maintenance projects without spreading them all over the chart table. And you will want to invite your children or friends to join you aboard as well. We wished that we had bought the CSY-44 when she first came out; she was no more expensive then than what we paid for her little sister, a CSY-37, a couple of years later.

The second piece of advice would be: Don't stint on ground tackle. Time and again we encountered boats that bashed into other vessels or ended up on the reefs because they had improper or inadequate anchors. One couple we encountered in the Bahamas lived aboard a ferro-cement vessel they had spent eleven years building (they had aptly named her *Patient Lady*). But they refused to spring for adequate ground tackle and became the scourge of every anchorage they entered. They gave up the sailing life after six months, and we breathed a collective sigh of relief.

Even if Martha's cancer had not returned, I think we would have ended this phase of our lives. It had been an enormously rewarding forty-two months, and we wouldn't have missed them for anything. We had made many good friends, thoroughly enjoyed their company, and kept up with many of them by radio even after we swallowed the anchor. But our whole existence had centered around boating; the main topics of conversation were fuel injectors, engine parts, and how to tenderize conch. We were more concerned about weather patterns and the tracks of tropical depressions, than about US and Soviet machinations. After a 3 ½ year hiatus, it really was time to rejoin the world.

***

Martha died in 1986, and I lost my anchor. Her cancer had metastasized and cropped up in many new places. But just before she died she made a comment that just blew me away. She said, "I wouldn't wish cancer on anyone, least of all on myself," she said, "but if I had to choose between cancer and a nervous breakdown, cancer would win hands down."

I was stunned. Speechless. I could only think of the many times I had become angry and impatient with her bipolar condition. The number of times I had shouted at her and had become short-tempered. Now, at last, I realized how totally devastating her manic-depressive episodes had been. But now it was too late — too late for anything but a profound sense of sadness and shame.

✿✿✿

5

The Year of the Umbrella

I had a hard time adjusting to Martha's death. We had been married for 35 years, had shared so much, been through so much and weathered so many crises together. I loaded up the *Mirage*, sailed down past Key Largo and Plantation Key, then turned north toward the uninhabited islands and the bird sanctuaries. There I dropped the hook and spent the better part of a fortnight reliving portions of our life, alternately cringing in self-recrimination and laughing over memories of her of her dry wit. Even when she was in the depths of her depressions, she'd manage some wry, self-deprecating humor:

"My mouth feels like the bottom of a birdcage," she'd say after taking some of her vile tasting medicine. Or, "I feel like I have to look up to a worm."

I had our books aboard, the ones we particularly cherished and would read to one another. Elizabeth Barrett Browning's *Sonnets from the Portuguese*, lines from which we had had engraved inside our wedding bands: *"How do I love thee? Let me count the ways...."* And *Anna Karenina* and Martha's college *Shakespeare* text, which she had covered with so many underlines and margin notes that it was a challenge to read. She had loved opera, and we had many tapes on board, but sea air is not kind to audio cassettes, and many of them delaminated, because we had played them so often.

I sailed on to Marathon, scattered some ashes in the harbor in which we had anchored so often, waiting for weather that would allow us to cross the Gulf Stream. I scattered some more of them in front of our (former) home, in Washington, where she had also spent her childhood, and when our children came down to Miami for a memorial service, scattered the remainder in the Atlantic that had treated us with such tolerance.

***

In an attempt to regain some direction, I immersed myself in a slew of projects, but without much success. Sidney Poittier's performance in *The*

Slender Thread inspired me to volunteer for Miami's Crisis Help line, but I didn't have any of Poittier's life-saving experiences; mostly the people who called were widows in their late 70s, living alone on Miami Beach, who just needed someone to talk to.

A local TV station hired me as the assistant to the producer of a morning talk show, and after a few weeks decided to give me a screen test as an understudy for the show's host. The director put it more kindly, but the message was clear: I was more effective *off*-camera – the further off the better.

I capitalized on my 30 years of CIA experience to become a consultant to businesses worried about industrial espionage. Except for one interesting case that took me to New York, the inquiries I received were overwhelmingly from individuals who wanted to know how to circumvent wire taps by the Drug Enforcement Administration or the IRS. I really didn't want any part of that scene, and closed the business down. I was appointed the Director of Crime Watch for southern Dade County, but instead of crime declining, it increased.

Prior to the mid-term elections of 1986, one of my Crime Watch captains called to seek an assurance that I would be voting Republican. Her husband was running for office.

"I'm not sure," I replied, "I think of myself as an Independent, and I think I'll be voting for a Democrat this year."

"Well, Carlos I don't know how you Cubans can vote anything but Republican – after all we've done for you."

"I'm not Cuban," I informed her politely, "despite a Hispanic name. In fact, I was born and raised in Germany."

"All the more reason. After all we've done for you Germans, you should be voting Republican, too!"

"Und vatt," I finally exploded, adopting my best German accent, "eggsactly haff you tun for uss? You bompt our sitees to smizzereens, drofe our gretest liter sinz Bismarck to sewiside, und zen gafe haff our kuntry to ze Russians. Vatt haff you tun for us?"

The lady never missed a beat. "I would remind you," she said, icily, "that all of that happened under Democratic administrations."

***

Then I came home one afternoon and discovered I had a new neighbor: a gorgeous 24 year old redhead had moved in next door, and was in her driveway, washing her car. Her name was Jenny, and she was very nicely filling a Swarthmore T-shirt.

I was stunned. Swarthmore? That tiny, 1,200 student Quaker college outside of Philadelphia? The Swarthmore College that had fired its football coach because he was winning too many games? The liberal Swarthmore College that Spiro T. Agnew had once called *'the Kremlin on the Crum,'* and that had had the gross misfortune of having had me as a student? *That* Swarthmore College?

Trying not to be too obvious about ogling her T-shirt, I sidled up to her and asked, disparagingly: "Swarthmore? That's a *girl's* school, isn't it?" For that was the question I was most frequently asked.

Jenny coolly regarded her 60-year old, overweight and obviously lecherous new neighbor, and patiently explained that *Skidmore* was the girl's school, while *Swarthmore* was a co-educational Quaker college.

"Oh," I replied. "And is Crum Creek still the co-eds doom?"

Jenny blinked; her eyes became round as saucers, and she dropped her sponge: "You're a *Swarthmoron,*" she asked, incredulously? Which is how I got to meet her mother.

The clouds parted and gradually vanished. I knew at once that she was an extraordinary woman, but I wasn't ready for a new relationship; my wife had died just nine months before. And having just escaped from a very bad marriage, a new entanglement was about the furthest thing from Sharon's mind as well. Still, we discovered that we shared the same values, bled over the same injustices, and enjoyed the same activities. Sharon too had been pursued by CIA while in college, but had turned them down. Of the hundreds of apartment complexes in Washington, we had lived in the same one -- though at different times. Our daughters had been born in the same small hospital in Alexandria, though years apart. We had both lived in and had friends in the town of Swarthmore, and now we were thrust together as neighbors.

Timing was everything. Had we both been single, thirty years earlier, we would not have hit it off. We were two driven, goal-oriented people. We had strong opinions on just about everything. We were both intensely competitive, and our clashes would have been frequent and noisy. Thirty years earlier I still had a lot of maturing to do, but now, maybe, I was grown up enough for a woman of Sharon's caliber. Besides, the Gods were becoming impatient. They were saying: "Enough already; it's time you two got together."

✿✿✿

6

SHARON

A year later we are married; in a Quaker ceremony. At Swarthmore. But with my background in particular, it is simply inexcusable that I didn't check her out more carefully before I proposed, for she has some really weird qualities.

Several months before we were married, we were sailing on Biscayne Bay when our 37' sloop began to sink. Two electrical and one manual bilge pumps had all failed and we were taking on water. Sharon can't swim; even at the beach she is terrified if the water is above her waist. If she'd had the brains that God gave a mule, you'd think that she would have thrown her arms around me and begged me to save her!

But she didn't. She merely grabbed the ship's bucket and began to bail, while I ran the vessel up on a sandbar until we could locate and fix the problem.

Sharon doesn't panic. There's something a little unsettling about people who don't panic, and we try to keep that character flaw of hers well hidden..

And then there's that curiosity of hers: Insatiable. She's always poking her nose into places that are none of her business. Like, four summers ago, when we were in The Hague, we came across a pretty little square that had a church on one side and a walled courtyard of little houses on the other.

They were called Alms houses and had been built a century or so earlier to house the very poor. The theory, I suppose, is that if you park the indigent very close to a church, it will keep them out of trouble.

But that was long ago, and today we realize that you don't squander prime real estate on the poor; the little dwellings have been gentrified, and now sell for a fortune. Indeed, the courtyard was in considerably better shape than the church that had spawned it.

Traffic in and out of the courtyard was brisk, but predominantly males – and they looked both surprised and a bit annoyed that Sharon was so furiously snapping pictures. Suddenly she decided that she needed to see what was going on in there, and with me hot on her heels, still trying to dissuade her, she burst into the courtyard.

It was a courtyard of window-shopping males, and the women on display were scantily clad at best. As Sharon was better looking than a number of the local specimens, she attracted an immediate following, while I was invited to leave, as I had entered without paying the entrance fee.

You'd think she would have learned her lesson, but in Merida, Yucatan, a year later, she ventured into another courtyard – only because its wrought iron gate was not firmly shut. It was the headquarters of the region's secret police, and they threw us out unceremoniously.

Once, I will admit, her curiosity paid off. We were cycling through the little village of Bloehmendaal, a pretty suburb of the Dutch city of Arnhem. Another unlocked gate and a courtyard enclosing a lovely garden. Sharon had to investigate, and the owner's dog came bounding out, followed by the lady of the house.

But instead of being irritated, she invited us in, gave us tour of her home, then drove us to the seaside resort of Scheveningen for tea. Her husband was minister of something in the government, which meant that they received tickets to all of the major openings. She gave us tickets to the Van Gogh exhibit at the stunning Kroller-Mueller Museum, and to a recital inaugurating the restored 17th Century organ in Arnhem's cathedral.

***

Read Bill Bryson's *A Walk in the Woods*, and you'll conclude that only lunatics attempt to thru-hike the Appalachian Trail. They typically start in Georgia in the early spring, and don't reach Maine until the first snows are dusting Mt. Katahdin.

Sharon is squarely in that category: -- certifiably insane. When Hurricane Andrew drops a tree on our home in Miami and we join the long queue of those standing in line for repairs, she announces that it would be a good opportunity to realize a life-time dream.

"Are you out of your mind? You want to *hike* the Appalachian Trail? Like on *foot?*" She nods.

"But it is 2,140 miles long," I complain. "More even, because you have to leave the Trail every week or so to hike into town and re-provision."

The fact is, I hate walking. Always have. I'm sure that somewhere in the Bible it is written that the ability to invent automobiles and motels was one of God's great gifts to man – and if it isn't, it was an oversight.

But we have only been married five years, and the bloom is still on the rose. We compromise, as we always do – which is to say that she gets her way. We agree that *she* will hike the Appalachian Trail, along with another certified nut and a very large dog, named Abber, while *I* will sensibly follow a parallel course in a van, stay in motels every night and collect stories for a book about the Appalachian corridor.

Every Friday I will meet the ladies at a point where the AT crosses a highway and – keeping well upwind of them, of course – will drive them to a motel for a bath. They will rest and re-provision on Saturday, and on Sunday I will deposit them again on the Trail.

Because winter has lasted much longer than usual, the two women start their trek at the Delaware Water Gap and head south; they will tackle the northern half of the Trail later in the summer. And that is why today, April 16th, 1993, I am waiting on Hawk Mountain in Pennsylvania, where the Appalachian Trail crosses the Hawk Mountain Rd.

It is a cold, blustery afternoon and patches of snow and ice still cling to the outcroppings. In fact, just three weeks before, a group of twenty-four thru-hikers had to be air-lifted out of the Great Smokies National Park when they were snowed in by a late winter storm.

The ladies are an hour behind schedule, but I'm not worried; they are hiking a particularly challenging stretch of the AT this week. I slump down with my book, glance idly at my side-view mirror – and freeze:

A tall, gaunt figure is standing motionless behind the van!

I hadn't heard him approach, and have no idea how long he may have been standing there. He reminds me of the Watusi of Central Africa you see pictured in the National Geographic – tall, solitary figures that remain rooted to one spot, seemingly for hours at a time. He is black, rail-thin, close to seven feet tall, and radiates an air of infinite calm. He is dressed in a brown robe, has a long stave in one hand, and what looks like a fuel pump in the other. He makes no move to address me -- in fact, I'm not even sure he realizes the vehicle is occupied, for I had slumped down in my seat.

When I get out and speak to him, he smiles gently and introduces himself. He says his name is Kwame, and that he's a prophet.

"A prophet?"

He hands me a dog-eared business card, and sure enough, it says *Kwame the Prophet.* I start to put it in my pocket, but he takes it back;

"It's my last one," he says.

Kwame tells me that he is fasting. "Last year I fasted forty days and forty nights," he says; "this year I'm tryin' for fifty." He's been at it for over two weeks and it's been damned cold.

"You are going without food and water for fifty days?"

He tells me that he is allowed one spare meal a day. And water. He has pitched a pup tent in a nearby a grove, has a small kerosene burner, a 5 gallon can of kerosene, a bedroll and some canned foods. Once a week he hikes five miles west to a general store in Drehersville to replenish his canned goods.

"You must make quite a stir in that outfit," I say.

"Oh, they kidded me some last year, but by now they's used to me."

A homeless person, I think to myself, and probably a mental case. But he strikes me as very gentle, and while his story is bizarre, it is delivered in a matter-of-fact and rational manner.

"You can make a living as a prophet?" I ask; he shakes his head.

"It's not a job," he tells me. "I'm a gardener and groundskeeper for a rich widow in Harrisburg. Only sometimes I get visions."

"Visions."

"Yeah. Like one day this lady come home, and I could see she been cryin'. She tell me I'd best be lookin' for other work."

"'What's the matter, m'am,' I ax her, for I'd knowed this lady for many years; 'I done somethin' to displease you?'

"She shake her head and say she been to see her doctor. He tell her she have a cancer and don't have long to live.

"In that moment I knowed he was wrong. I jest knowed it!" He says he grabbed her by the shoulders, and looked deep into her eyes. She was surprised; he was surprised himself, for he had never touched her before, but he had this overwhelming conviction.

"'You lissen to me, m'am,' he said earnestly, 'that doctor he be wrong. It ain't your time, yet; you hear me? You got years to live.' That was ten years ago," he adds, "and I been workin' for her ever since."

He can see I'm still skeptical. "My sister, Jean," he says, "she have two kids in school? I calls her last year, and tells her: 'you get them kids outta school, right away; somethin' terrible's gonna happen!' 'Yeah, like what?' she ax me, only I don't know. She say she can't take off from work on some crazy hunch, and hang up,

"But that afternoon a kid bring his daddy's gun to school and starts shootin' up the place. One teacher and two kids wounded -- maybe you read about it? Jean's kid was OK, but she tole the pohleece that I had called her, and they wanted to know how I knowed."

"What did you tell them?"

"I tells 'em I jest had a feelin'; they don't believes me and keeps pushin', but I'm tellin' the truth, and eventually they lets me go.

A police cruiser passes us, stops and backs up to check what is going on. When he sees it's Kwame, he smiles and waves. "You keepin' from freezin' your ass, he asks? Kwame salutes him with his staff, and the patrolman drives on.

The women are now almost two hours overdue, and it will soon be dark. They don't have enough food or water with them for another night, and the impending storm is just going to add to their misery.

"Don't worry," Kwame assures me, "they be OK." I ask him whether he is having another one of his 'feelings' and he shrugs and shakes his head.

Kwame had been dropped off by his sister, along with a supply of food and fuel. He shows me how he has dammed a gully to trap rain water; because of the heavy rain and melting snow his reservoir is a good six feet across and a foot deep. He shows me his meager larder, and I offer to share some of our food with him, but he declines. He'd sure like some cigarettes, though, he says; he gave up smoking about the time he had started his fast, and that was a mistake. "I shoulda done one or the other," he says; "but not both."

In fact, he's about ready to give up the whole thing, because it's so cold. He gives me his sister Jean's phone number and asks me to call her and have her pick him up. I try with my cell phone, but up here, in the mountains, there are no towers nearby and the thing is useless.

It will be dark before long, and I'm really getting worried. A number of hikers are ham radio operators, as I am, and I had long since put out a call for anyone who might have spotted the two women. But to no avail. Kwame offers to go look for them, and at first I demur; but then I figure he knows these woods better than most.

I warn him about the dog, however: the two women have encountered some unsavory characters on the AT, and each time the dog has planted himself directly in their path, growled menacingly and bared his fangs until Ann has given him the OK. But Kwame dismisses the warning; animals love him, he assures me, as he sets off down the trail.

He finds them twenty minutes later. They had missed one of the Appalachian Trail's blazes, had taken a wrong turn and had realized their mistake. They are on the way back and rounding a bend when they encounter a gaunt, black figure who calls them by name. Rather than growl, Abber wags his tail furiously.

That night I try four times to reach Jean, from the motel, but there's no answer. I call again the next morning, and when a woman answers, ask to speak to Jean,

"Yeah? Who wants her?" she asks belligerently, and I pass on Kwame's message.

"That crazy nigger!" she says, and slams down the phone.

***

There are no accommodations on the Appalachian Trail – not in the real sense. There are lean-tos every ten or fifteen miles, occasional privies, and places where water bottles can be topped up. But little else. Over time the lean-tos rot or fall apart and sometimes a local club will construct a new one, or the hikers simply do without.

Two weeks or so have passed since the encounter with Kwame. Winter storms have made a mess of the Trail; trees are down, blocking their path, and blazes have become obscured. The ladies are cold and they are sore; the sky looks threatening, and they are still five miles from the next shelter. Sharon's map, however, shows an abandoned shelter a half mile to the south of the Trail.

They shoulder their 35 lb. packs and set off along a narrow, winding path that threads its way downward through a thick tangle of underbrush. But the further they progress, the more apprehensive they become. An unnatural stillness surrounds them, as though the forest is holding its breath. Perhaps it is the lowering sky, or the chill invading their parkas, but they sense a sinister quality, a furtiveness, an air of quiet menace to this isolated spot.

The instincts that animals possess never cease to amaze me. As they near the abandoned shelter, their dog, Abber plants himself firmly in their path. The hair rises on the back of his neck; he growls as they press on and pulls back furiously on his leash.

The lean-to, or what is left of it, is in a clearing. Tendrils of fog are invading the hollow, and the area has a brooding, malevolent quality to it, as though it is a place where spirits lurk, and bide their time.

Within the lean-to they find a rough-hewn table, and pinned to it a zip-lock bag containing a note and a picture of a laughing young couple. Now yellowing around the edges but still quite legible, the letter it contains was written by a young woman whose brother was murdered there two years earlier.

As I hiked from Duncannon to this Shelter today, I really did not know what my feelings would be, at this place, where my brother Geoffrey and my dear friend, Molly, had taken their last breaths. I had expected to feel sorrow and anger, where one man's actions altered the course of my life forever.

Instead, what I find myself experiencing is a sense of peace, and it surprises me. As I look around I can see dark stains of what I suppose must be their blood, and it is very difficult not to visualize what happened on that day and to feel the pain that they experienced. But instead I believe I am sensing the peace that they ultimately found.

I love you, Geoff and Molly, and I will miss you as long as I live. May peace be with those that pass this way.

(name withheld)
Thelma Marks Shelter
May 19ᵗʰ, 1992.

It is too dark to continue; too late to try to find another place to pitch their tents. They spend the night in the clearing, but neither of them sleep.

***

She denies it, of course, but I'm sure that the Pied Piper was one of Sharon's close relatives. She certainly possesses his empathy for children and they are drawn to her as moths to a candle flame.

A few years ago we were in Mexico on an exchange program, visiting a dirt-poor barrio. The children flocked around her, laughing and telling her all about their adventures. Sharon doesn't speak a word of Spanish, and the children spoke no English, but that didn't matter. Her body language was enough; the light in her eyes was enough; the way she gathered them up in her arms and hugged them - that was enough. It has always been thus: me they tolerate; her they adore.

Children are her passion, particularly the young and defenseless that are dealt a rotten hand. Before their experiences, their neighborhoods or their parents bend them out of shape, she is convinced that they have a capacity and a hunger to learn. But too often that potential remains un-fulfilled.

With the encouragement and support of the County's school super-intendent, she launched a program called *All Aboard* that paired children at risk with caring volunteers who coached them in subjects that were giving them trouble. She began with just a few of her friends, but within a very short time had recruited an army of over 100 volunteers, including a num-ber of Child Development majors from nearby Clemson University. She set up training courses for her volunteers, and recruited experts from all over the state to conduct periodic In-Service programs. She deployed her troops to all of the county's primary schools, to work one-on-one with children in Kindergarten through the 4th grade that were deemed to be at risk.

Of even greater concern to her are the children forcibly removed from their homes because of parental neglect or abuse. Police and well-meaning social workers take them away, but all of a sudden their entire world is turned on its ear. The state has its laws to protect; the parents have rights they believe have been violated, and the defenseless child is caught in the meat grinder, between the two.

Sharon joined the Guardian ad Litem program and herself has become a guardian. She fights for her charges like a tigress, and has been instrumental in finding good, adoptive homes for many of them. Once, when a state agency balked at providing medical treatment that one of her wards required, she took the agency to court, and won. On yet another occasion, when a convicted felon, serving a ten year sentence for aggravated assault refused to give up his parental rights, purely out of spite, she drove 120 miles to the prison, talked to him for an hour and secured the necessary release. .

But as is so often the case, the good die young. Sharon died in May, 2006 -- three months shy of her 70th birthday -- of endometrial cancer. She had battled breast cancer successfully, ten years earlier, and there wasn't a trace of it left in her system, but the fight against this second onslaught she lost.

When we sorted through her stuff, we found a small envelope in her golf bag containing $1.80 – it was her 'prize money' for birdying the #3 hole; she had played that round just eleven days before she died.

Someday, if I live long enough, I shall write about her -- about her generous nature and her sensitivity to people. About her awesome organizational skills that reduced the most complex problems to manageable bits. About her devotion to family, and about the joy with which she filled our lives. She enriched everyone she touched. She was a gutsy woman; she was an extraordinary woman, and her story needs to be told.

We were married in 1987 – it seems like just the day before yesterday. I would never have believed that nineteen years could pass so quickly.

✳✳✳

EPILOGUE

Those of us who served in CIA during the Cold War sometimes ask ourselves: was it worth it? The billions of dollars spent, the thousands of lives risked and the many lost? Much as we might like to think so, we didn't really 'win' the Cold War -- the other guys lost it. They ran out of money; they ran out of steam; their system collapsed because it rotted from within – gutted by appalling levels of corruption. Wouldn't it have happened of its own accord?

We can't ever know, can we? But can a nation's leaders take the chance? If it is true that nature abhors a vacuum, is that not also true of geo-politics?

Our nemesis in Europe was Markus Wolf – head of East Germany's Foreign Intelligence branch. (Though not in true name, he in fact appears as a pivotal character in John Le Carré's *The Spy Who Came in from the Cold*). His was among the best of the professional Intelligence services in the area, certainly equal to, and some would say superior to the Soviets, the British and our own.

Reflecting upon his career in 1997, Dr. Wolf said:

CARLOS D. LURIA

"The intelligence services of East & West have contributed to over half a century of peace -- the longest Europe has ever known. They gave their statesmen the security that they would not be surprised by the other side."

That, perhaps, is an adequate legacy. For all of us.

Salem, SC
September 19th , 2006

END NOTES

[1] National Highway Traffic Safety Board, Report for 2004

[2] While Dr. Schacht was anti-Semitic, he was also strongly opposed to the mistreatment of the Jews. Hitler fired him in 1939, and Schacht was cleared of all charges at the Nuremberg Trials. See http://www.spartacus. schoolnet.co.uk/GERschacht.htm

[3] *The Rubaiyat of Omar Khayyam, Edward Fitzgerald's 1859 Translation*

[4] The complete specifications for this aircraft may be found at http:// www.fas.org/irp/program/collect/u-2.htm

[5] *Battleground Berlin,* David E. Murphy, Sergei A. Kondrashev and George Bailey, ISBN 0-300-07233-3

[6] Ministerium fuer Staatsicherheit – the German Democratic Republic's Intelligence and Security Service

[7] George Washington Univ. National Security Archives, Interview of 1/31/98 http://tinyurl.com/dskac

[8] The goals and methodology of the VANESSA project are accurate, though its name and the events leading up to it have been fictionalized The testimony before the Church Committee has been reconstructed, but is substantially correct. A letter addressed to a Mr. Frank Church from the Soviet Union was indeed opened. we'd like think that if it had been addressed to Sen. Frank Church it would have been passed, but the over-worked technicians didn't pay much attention to the addressees. In any event, it was so sloppily resealed that he became suspicious; that led to the unraveling of the project.

[9] For a full account of this and other cases in which TSD's disguise techniques played significant roles, see Tony Mendez' *Master of Disguise*, ISBN 075675125X

[10] http://www.pbs.org/wgbh/nova/spiesfly/brugioni.html

[11] For a full account of this case, see Benjamin Weiser's gripping *A Secret Life*, ISBN 1-891620-54-1

[12] http://www.cia.gov/csi/studies/vol47no3/article02.html#author#author

[13] *The Sorry State of the CIA*, by Reuel Marc Gerecht, see http://www.aei.org/publications/pubID.20911/pub_detail.asp

[14] http://www.edwardjayepstein.com/archived/spywars_print.htm

[15] *State of War, the Secret History of the CIA and the Bush Administration*

[16] The Tonkin Gulf Resolution, http://www.fair.org/media-beat/940727.html

Made in the USA